Generous Faith

STORIES TO INSPIRE ABUNDANT LIVING

Sister Bridget Haase, OSU

PARACLET

BREWSTER, MASSAC

Generous Faith: Stories to Inspire Abundant Living

2013 Third Printing
2009 First and Second Printing

ISBN 978-1-55725-615-7

Scripture references marked NAB are taken from the *New American Bible with Revised New Testament and Revised Psalms* © 1991, 1986, 1970 Confraternity of Christian Doctrine, Washington, D.C. and are used by permission of the copyright owner. All rights reserved.

Scripture references marked NRSV are taken from the *New Revised Standard Version of the Bible,* copyright 1989, 1995 by the Division of Christian Education of the National Council of Churches of Christ in the United States of America and are used by permission. All rights reserved.

Library of Congress Cataloging-in-Publication Data
Haase, Bridget, 1942-
  Generous faith : stories to inspire abundant living / Bridget Haase.
     p. cm.
  ISBN 978-1-55725-615-7
1. Christian life. I. Title.
  BV4515.3.H33 2009
  242—dc22   2009012938

10 9 8 7 6 5 4 3

Published by Paraclete Press
Brewster, Massachusetts
www.paracletepress.com

Printed in the United States of America

WITH GRATITUDE TO MY

Ursuline Sisters around the world,
each with a story to tell

CONTENTS

If you're like me and countless others, the question, *Is this all there is to life?* creeps up from time to time. Challenging both philosophers and prophets, the question weaves itself into the basic building blocks of our everyday lives. This haunting question may invade our thoughts at a new home act-of-sale, or at a job promotion party, or at a tragic death, or even at a family picnic. In these moments what we have always wanted, or perhaps what we have most feared, seems to stop us in our tracks and dull our hearts with a sense of incompleteness and subtle meaninglessness.

Hungering for this elusive "more" in life, we waste time and energy in a quixotic search for deeper meaning. We look in the nooks and crannies of life to satisfy our desires or assuage this sense of emptiness. We are left with the feeling that life has short-changed us and has offered us far less than we had hoped for. We begin to anxiously measure our life by the years we have left and panic when we find ourselves caught in a subtle web of discontent and imperfect answers.

While *Generous Faith: Stories to Inspire Abundant Living* will not take away your search or eradicate your feelings, my hope is that this book of stories will satisfy some of your hunger, revitalize your energy, and surprise you at what is right there under your feet. I am convinced that this *is* all there is to life and it *is* quite enough, for in the air we breathe, and in this very moment, the abundant life is available to us.

In order to cultivate this awareness, I offer three basic practices: living in the moment; trusting in divine care; and experiencing God's presence.

This book is not a how-to guide containing methods, techniques, or even a list of do's and don'ts. Neither is this book a manual of exercises to complete, nor an easy step-by-step program for instant success. Rather, here is a collection of stories that will open your heart to these three practices, giving shape and face to the abundant life.

Although these stories are about other people's lives, they may mirror your own journey. They are presented without explanation or evaluation, but they will challenge you to reexamine the path of *your* life. The power in these stories will not only evoke your experiences, but they will also transform you as you find them changing your perspective on your daily life. As you meet these people and think about their stories and reflect upon your life, you may be astounded to discover how abundant your life already is.

As you spend time with these spiritual tutors and personal trainers, you will begin to connect the dots and see how your past, personal encounters and experiences frame the person you are today. You will understand that a passing conversation with a stranger can powerfully reveal a mutual search for meaning in life. You will realize that we do not need to seek abundant life anywhere else. It is right here, right now, under our feet, and in the air we breathe.

This *is* all there is to life and it really *is* quite enough.

You may be puzzled at the title of this book. You may even be curious as to why the word *generous* is used to complement the word *faith*. If you find this an unusual coupling of words, perhaps this will pique your interest and set your wheels in motion to think more deeply about your own spiritual life.

The word *generous* originally comes to us, by way of the Old French, from the Latin word for noble stock. Its characteristics are courage, magnanimity, a largesse that implies a larger-than-life vision. With this understanding as a backdrop, we will meet people who flesh out the meaning of what generous faith is all about. These people believe in their divine noble stock as children of God; they see in the dark and give big-heartedly until it hurts; they trust beyond all odds and rejoice in ordinary things. Living beyond mere optimism, they exude the grace and the hope of the abundant life that is under their feet.

This title asks us to go one step further. "Generous faith" impels us to mine, with integrity, fortitude, and abundance, the faith within each of us. By digging deeply, we will discover a reservoir of divine marvels, and we will come to realize that we are to offer a lavish, reciprocal response. In so doing, we will enrich our own lives and the lives of others as the people in these stories did.

━◦═◦═━

This book is divided into three parts. Each section follows the same format: a reflection on a practice for the abundant life; a collection of real-life stories, each ending with questions to help you mine your own faith and to enrich your own life; and a series of short "pauses" that will take you a minute to read but days to digest.

You may wonder how I came to categorize each story, since stories are not meant to fit under tight titles or to be compartmentalized. Ultimately, I let the stories speak to me and, in a way, they arranged themselves. You may believe that some of the stories fit in more than one category, because you are tapping into more than one of the story's many levels.

PART ONE explores the first practice of the abundant life: an attention to living in the moment.

People often ask, "How do I really live in the present?" The answer is neither mysterious nor elusive. We are simply called to use our five senses of tasting, hearing, touching, seeing, and smelling to experience the "now"—the fullness of this specific moment in time. Our senses bring us to the simple awareness of the here and now and help us experience the fullness of what we are, as we are, where we are, without judgment. We may smack our lips with Josefina as we savor a warm tortilla oozing with cheese—and taste the abundant life. Beside Sister Mary Xavier, we will reverently contemplate a summer starburst sky and be overwhelmed by a feeling of fecundity.

PART TWO examines the second practice of the abundant life: accepting and trusting in divine care.

As we live in the present moment, we allow the moment to unfold and blossom in its own way. With a trusting heart, we surrender in trust to divine care, confidently casting our daily cares upon God because we know God provides for us. Under a shade tree, we find ourselves sitting next to Appalachian Bird as he shares what makes life "mighty fine." Or we may examine our desires to be acknowledged and honored as we share Nicky's forgotten birthday behind prison bars.

PART THREE brings us to the third practice of the abundant life: experiencing God's presence in our everyday life.

Living with attention in the present moment and accepting its unfolding as both a sign and an experience of divine care foster the attitude of belief that each moment, each person, and each event bears the footprints of the Divine. We begin to see with the eyes of Delena and Elam who, in sharing a Thanksgiving dinner with a church lady, rejoice that Jesus has come to their home. We become aware, as my mother did, of God's face reflected in gardenias and Pine-Sol-cleaned floors.

While there are many ways to use this book, here is one approach you may find particularly beneficial: beginning with the three practices, THE FIRST STEP is to spend time, perhaps a few days, recalling how living in the moment, trusting in divine care, and experiencing God's presence may already be an integral part of your life.

Be specific as you recall moments when your senses called your attention to the here and now. Ponder how these experiences unfolded and nudged you to greater trust in divine care and to an increased awareness of God's presence. Then thoughtfully read each essay through the lens of your own past experiences. A sharper vision of what already exists in your own life prepares you for the next step.

THE SECOND STEP is to attentively read each story, perhaps aloud in front of your fireplace or quietly at your kitchen table. To avoid feeling like an onlooker, savor the story from the inside out. By doing this, you may discover that you and the person in the story have had similar experiences—that you think alike—even ask the same questions about life's values and choices. Above all, take your time with each story, with even a second or third read-through. Slowly, carefully, let its power take hold of you and offer you another glimpse of your abundant life.

An important word of caution. Your first reaction to some stories may be to wonder how you can identify with them. Perhaps you cannot imagine Aisha's life in a refugee camp in the desert of Sudan; or share Preacher Nevins Ellis's religious beliefs and practices; or even understand Julia's compromised world of AIDS. Do not make the mistake of limiting your own personal engagement in these stories. The geography and situation of your life may differ, but your heart, with its same hungers and language, has a similar landscape. If you openly cross the cultural borders of these stories, you will be surprised to discover that Aisha's reverence for water deepens your appreciation. As Preacher Nevins Ellis did, you may examine your own depth of faith in God's Word. In meeting Julia, you may look on a cranky neighbor's physical challenge with greater acceptance and compassion.

THE THIRD STEP is to ponder the reflection questions that follow each story. Take time to use these questions to mine your own faith and enrich your life. Mull over the questions when you find yourself stuck in traffic, or while taking a break at the water cooler, or baking birthday cupcakes. As you meditate, you may discover that what happened in each particular encounter is also occurring in your own life. You can even take this reflection a step further by choosing a word or phrase from the story. Let it become a mantra—a word of wisdom to encourage and inspire you as you go about your daily routine.

Equally as important as the other three, THE FOURTH STEP requires a slow, steady pace: reflecting on the "short pauses." Because they are brief and easily read, the temptation may be to gulp them down in one sitting. Beware. Doing so will result in spiritual indigestion. You will find it more beneficial to think of each short pause as a panoramic snapshot of life. Take time to measure its depth; focus on its perspective; and study it from different angles. Finally, frame it with your own meaning and experience.

However you read *Generous Faith: Stories to Inspire Abundant Living*, I hope you will discover a Mr. Ferguson in your neighborhood or chuckle as you realize that you are a lot like Bird, for whom nature was enough. Above all, I hope this book evokes memories and encourages conversations about how you have lived in the moment, trusted in divine care, and experienced God's presence. Then you may want to take a second look at your life and discover that this *is* all you have. Smiling broadly, you will realize that it is *more* than enough since it is, quite simply, most abundant.

PART ONE
Living in the Moment

For most of my life, living with attention in the present moment, the first practice of the abundant life, has been a challenge. I felt as though I was only respectfully saluting the "here and now"—doing it in a disengaged manner, hurriedly bowing as it passed by. The conviction that mystics and spiritual masters consider attentiveness to the moment the highest form of spirituality frustrated me even more. I sensed the rightness and importance of being attentive, but no one had shown me how to do it.

Then one summer day, while spoon-feeding my mother chocolate ice cream, I discovered how I *could* live in the present moment—sometimes we learn how to live from people who are dying.

My mama sat in her wheelchair, eyes glazed over and unable to speak. At eighty-three, she was aimlessly drifting on the ocean of Alzheimer's disease. Knowing she had forgotten how to swallow, I was slowly and carefully feeding her. Unexpectedly, she gestured as though trying to smack her lips.

"You like it, Mama?" I asked through the tears that welled up at such moments. I was expecting a smile, a response, a nod. None came from her, but a waterfall of memories cascaded over me.

I began to reminisce how, after supper dishes were done, Mama would get out the jelly jars and the Sealtest ice cream carton. My four siblings and I would dash into the kitchen, putting homework and squabbling aside. Chocolate ice cream was a built-in family reunion. Being alert for equal portions, we would then indulge, slurping until there was no sound but the spoon tapping the side of the glass. Hope for one last taste sprang eternal.

Mama never baked cookies or cakes. Once, when I asked her why, she very firmly said, "No need to when you've got chocolate ice cream." That ended the discussion and explained everything.

I returned from my reverie to reenter the reality of the Alzheimer's disease that was consuming her. How could someone, so brave, so heroic, and so active, be smitten with a disease that slowly robs both physical senses and mental abilities? Would Mama continue to deteriorate in the coming months? Would she feel pain—lose more dignity?

Pity for her overcame me, and I began to feel both anger and deep sadness. Dipping my spoon once again into the ice cream cup, I tapped Mama's cheek so she would open her mouth and remember to swallow.

Suddenly my memories and future worries were interrupted as a strange feeling engulfed me. I realized I had mentally crossed my personal International Date Line. I was straddling the present, one foot in the past and the other in the future. I had allowed the thoughts that chocolate ice cream evoked within me to distract me from the gift of this precious moment with Mama. Instead of simply enjoying the experience of being with Mama and feeding her, I had allowed myself to ruminate on the experience. In so doing, I had entered into another time zone. Mama, on the other hand, smacking her lips with the pleasurable taste of chocolate cream, was living totally in the present moment. I knew then that this was what I lacked, and for this I longed.

In Mama's ending, I discovered how to begin.

This first practice of the abundant life is to make a deliberate choice: namely, to be aware of and sensitive to what our senses apprehend, to what we are experiencing, without imposing thoughts and commentary about it—experiencing what I am, being where I am, and not evaluating, judging, or weighing the merits. This practice allows us to live fully *in* the here and now without thinking *about* the moment. Simple awareness.

Awareness of where we are and attention to what is happening remind us that we do not need to be astronomers to be overcome by a starry night sky. We do not need to study combustion before we feel the warmth of a fire. Nor do we need to understand the digestive system in order to quench our thirst with the sweetness of water. What matters is that we see the person before us or feel what is around us. It's really that simple. To live *in* the moment is to *experience* the moment.

We, too, are created to savor and enjoy every moment of life. Unfortunately, we do just the opposite. When we shower, we plan the day's schedule rather than simply feel the rush of water upon our shoulders. When we smell a gardenia, we draw up future plans for a garden rather than just let the fragrance bless us. When we sit by a stream in a local park, we wish we were at a popular mountain resort, far away from our daily routine and duty, rather than hear the gurgling gift of flowing water. When we see flowering lilac bushes in the spring, do we begin summer vacation countdown or linger over the beauty of lilacs? When watermelon juice runs down our chin, do we wonder if mangoes would have tasted even better?

Living in the here and now demands daily discipline. It does not simply "happen." Being attentive to what surrounds and encompasses us takes a response of the will and a diligent awareness of our five senses. Our senses bring us to the here and now as we observe every detail and feel our physical setting. We become entirely present to what we see, hear, taste, touch, or smell. Nothing escapes us; everything speaks to us. Each one of our senses becomes a clue to the mystery of the present moment.

As we experience what is unfolding before us, we are like the young child who, walking with her mom in a garden nursery, called her mother over to see the brilliant colors of the gerbera daisies. Her mother, engrossed in her garden planning and vegetable list, nonchalantly responded, "Yes, I see them."

"No, you don't, Mommy," she whined. "Look NOW."

Her mother stopped short, and, peering over her reading glasses, leaned over the vivid blooms and gently cupped a flaming red daisy in her hand. All mental activity seemed to stop as she, in one intense moment of attention, *really* looked.

Acute listening can also anchor us in the power of the present. Being a teacher, I learned this lesson from one of my third graders. One warm, spring day, my students were playing kick ball, rhyming jump rope, and running wild as they were getting winter out of their bones. My eye caught Corey, sitting quietly alone on a wooden bench, lost in thought and staring straight ahead. It was unusual behavior for this dynamic and sensitive child. Certain that his feelings had been hurt, I sauntered over and sat down beside him. He didn't budge. Gently, I touched his arm and asked him what the matter was. He jerked out of his trance, smiled and whispered in his lisp, "Nothing, Sister, I was just listening to the boids." Sure enough, from a nearby bush, came melodious chirping and twittering. This eight-year-old was swept up in the symphony of the "now." I, his teacher, hadn't heard anything but the ringing of the five-minutes-left-to-recess bell.

Touch, too, can root us in the reality before us. During the famine of 1986, a young woman named Fatima came to our relief camp birthing center with its straw overhang, makeshift table, and dirt floor. She had walked across the Sudan desert suffering from enduring labor pains. Without a moan or wail, as is the cultural ritual, she gave birth to a crying baby girl. Emquoish, her sister and companion on the journey, immediately took the child and, with bare hands, began to clean the infant. She shook the slimy blood from her hands, never flinching as it stuck to her clothes and slid under her fingernails. Oblivious to its stain and smell, she, chanting and caressing, continued to soothe the infant and heal her trauma of leaving the womb. With her eyes riveted upon the child, Emquoish forgot about distended stomachs and parched lips just a few yards away. In seeing and feeling red, slippery blood, she was holding new life.

Sight can also bring us to attention. "You must see the Alps before you leave France," invited Sister Martine. "I know just the spot," she told me. Gathering the most physical energy I could as an inexperienced climber, I joined Martine, as we trekked up a short but winding path that she knew like the back of her hand.

I plopped breathless on an uneven rock and then glanced up. I gasped. It wasn't the snow-capped mountains, the gentle mist, or the mysterious aura of silence that nestled me in the here and now. It simply was the fact that these mountains *are* and I *am* in this precise moment.

To live deliberately with acute attention to our surroundings also means to be consciously aware of the odors and fragrances that encircle us. A few weeks into my service as a relief worker during the Sudan famine, a wave of cholera hit some of the children in the refugee camp. We immediately isolated them as best we could by cutting small holes in the cord beds so that the diarrhea could pass through onto the desert dirt floor. The smell coupled with that of the children's vomiting was overwhelming. To remain in the moment was our only choice. There was nowhere else to go. Smell held us captive, and there was nothing to do but experience the odor that linked life and death.

Allowing ourselves to truly engage our senses joins us to all people, cultures, and faiths. From Buddhism to Christianity, all the great religions witness to the extravagance of the present moment. Jesus, for example, teaches us to jump into our senses without evaluation. In the Gospels of Matthew and Luke, Jesus eats and drinks with sinners; tells us to look at the birds of the air and the lilies of the field; reminds us to use our ears to hear the divine message; offers a healing touch to both a leper and a servant with a severed ear; and in the Gospel of John he accepts Lazarus' stench of death. Jesus, engaging himself fully in the five human senses in each and every moment, shows us how to live life abundantly.

Living with attention in the present moment is a day-by-day discipline that sometimes takes us a lifetime to realize. But, in return, we suddenly hear a cardinal's whistle trumpeting the sunrise. We feel life even as we wipe a bloody nose, see a storm brewing on the horizon, smell our reeking compost pile, or taste the chocolate ice cream gliding down our dry, summer throats.

Blazing Fire
ON ATTENTION TO PASSION

When life seems like a pile of ashes, how might living in the here and now rekindle my passion?

He never knew his advice had implications far beyond the coal stove and the cold, Appalachian winter.

Summer brought out the copperheads in the woods across our creek, the dandelion greens we picked in the hills, and the lightning bugs galore visible in the cool of the evening. Dog days came and went. Gradually summer ended.

Frost coated the pumpkins. The air, so long heavy and thick, was crisp with fall freshness, and autumn leaves began their good-byes. With winter peeking around the corner, thoughts turned to chopping wood and preparing the coal box.

My beloved neighbor Mr. Ferguson took notice of the preparations. He would wander over, watching carefully as I sorted through the wood box to find pieces of wood to split for kindling. Flinging the axe, I would hit and then miss. Mr. Ferguson said nothing about these feeble attempts and small successes. He would, after some time, just stand up, shake his head, and softly mumble under his breath, "'Fraid not." Then he would saunter home.

The time came to stack wood on the porch for easy access on cold days. I paid no heed to separating pine from oak from hickory logs. Only experience would teach me that pine burned quickly, oak would simmer, and that bitterly cold days needed the long-burning hickory. To me, wood was wood.

Mr. Ferguson would again meander over, eye everything, say nothing. After a bit, he would get up, mumble once again and amble home.

Crisp frost gave way to snow and biting cold. Day after day, I would start a fire, tend it, shake the ashes, and try to bank it for the night. But the three-room house never warmed up. I just assumed that everyone shivers in Appalachian winters. After all, life is rugged, and coal stoves can only give out so much heat.

One December evening, Mr. Ferguson paid his regular neighborly visit. I invited him in. He sat close to the stove, rubbing his hands and face, graciously receiving my apology for my icy hands and home. As was his habit, he sat in silence and simple presence.

"The best words come slowly," he was prone to say.

Mustering my courage and swallowing my pride, I finally spoke. "Mr. Ferguson," I said, "there's something mighty wrong with this coal stove. I've been so cold and miserable for weeks.

What should I do?"

Suddenly, he rose with the dignity of a university president before a major address. A broad toothless smile came over his face and a Santa Claus twinkle was in his eye.

"At last you asked," he declared, rather than spoke. "Now I can help you. I am rightly pleased."

With the conviction of a preacher and the certainty born of many a mountain winter, he stated, "What you got here is nothin' but smolderin' ashes. You ain't got a real fire so you ain't got heat. You're gonna freeze before too long. Everything you need is inside this coal stove, but you got to learn your wood. You just got to make it work for you—to learn to tend and keep it. You got to live from a blazing fire, and not from some cold ashes. Then everything around you will feel warm."

When he said "blazing fire," I saw a spark shoot from the twinkle in his eyes. His secret was betrayed.

Detail by detail, he began to teach me the art of tending a fire, of caring for a coal stove, of splitting and stacking logs with attention and appreciation.

"Remember. Live from a blazing fire, not some cold ashes," he would say, as he stoked the fire in rhythm to his chant.

Three hard years later, on a frigid February day, this dear neighbor came for his regular weekly visit. Warmth penetrated the house as the fire crackled with its own melody. After some time, his face aglow, Mr. Ferguson rose slowly and deliberately, as he had on that cold night now long past. Breaking into his trademark toothless smile and rubbing his hands in contentment, he declared:

"Reckon I can say it now. You got the know-how of starting a fire, tending it, and warming everything around you. Now you're living from the fire, not just cold ashes. You know your wood, and you're making what you got work for you. I'm so honored to tell you. You're a real, one-hundred-percent hillbilly."

This old mountain man's flint of wisdom had sparked a fire within me. Could I believe that, like my coal stove, I have everything I need inside of me and I need only make it work? Could I live from a blazing fire and not cold ashes?

Fidelity to daily routine burns and consumes the best of us. Sometimes it seems easier to live from the cold ashes of yesterday's regrets or worries. Only if I live from a blazing fire—live my passion and follow it in the present moment—will everything around me be ignited.

MINING OUR FAITH, ENRICHING OUR LIFE

From what cold ashes of the past am I tempted to live? What "kindling" within me might spark a blazing fire and ignite a passion to live in the present moment?

SHORT PAUSE *Smack in the Middle*

Eight-year-old Nancy, an academically challenged student in my learning center, was always more interested in her lip gloss and her hairbrush than in remedial reading.

One day, she burst exuberantly into the center, "Sister," she blurted out, "I know exactly what happens when I pray."

With a sweeping gesture toward the heavens, she continued, "My heart goes up and God's heart comes down, and we meet smack in the middle."

Hearing those words, all my years of theology and all the books I had read on prayer seemed to pile up in a heap at my feet. In order to pray, I don't have to "find" God or wait until life is sorted out. God is smack in the middle of each moment and everything in life—be it gloss or tangle.

SHORT PAUSE *Snakes in the Attic*

It was a strange encounter.

I plopped in the nearest subway seat and the woman next to me scooted closer.

"Miss, got any snakes in your attic?" she asked.

"Not me."

"Sure you do," she persisted. "Everybody's got 'em. They slither and slide. Real annoying but harmless. It's the boa that you got to watch out for. That one can swallow you alive."

Oddly enough, this fellow commuter raised deeper questions within me about living in the present moment. I still ponder this strange encounter and unusual conversation as I ask myself, *What pointless anxieties and constant motion slither and slide in my life? Do past regrets and future worries swallow the life of the here and now?*

Do you have any snakes in your attic?

One-on-One

When a desperate situation calls us and stretches us
beyond our limits and abilities, what is the secret to living in
the present moment?

Our eyes were fixed on each other. Her eyes were dulled with the pangs of starvation; mine were hungry to know if she would have the strength to hold the cup of milk today. We were surrounded by hundreds of children, sitting on straw mats with hands outstretched for food. Flies stuck in their noses, ears, and hair, but the children were too weak even to swat them away. Cries for hot milk gave way to whimpers and wails. Here in the midst of the children of famine, it had taken me a long time to discover the importance of reaching out to the one child in front of me. I had come to realize that if I focused on a crowd of starving children and hundreds of needy refugees, and did not see individuals, my service would be impersonal, distant, and perhaps, uncaring.

We never know when life—or maybe God—will stretch us beyond our perceived limits. My moment came on a Wednesday night in spring while I was watching a BBC television special on the 1985 famine in Sudan.

The filmmaker had zoomed in on a feeding center in the desert. Three times, a child stretched out her small, thin hands for bread. Three times, a relief worker, his attention stretched beyond its limits, bypassed her.

As I was to learn later on when I worked for a relief organization and fed hundreds of children a day, skipping a child was an easy mistake to make. Relief workers had to retrace their steps over and over. But at the time, in front of the television, I did not realize this and found myself fervently praying, "God, give her something to eat." I went to bed hoping that God would answer my prayer.

The next morning, the image of the starving child still captivated my mind and heart. Yet, as happens over the course of a night's sleep, the impact of that child on the television lessened in my mind. Thoughts of the demanding routine of the day ahead—teaching challenged students and an afternoon teachers' meeting—assuaged my guilt as I relished cold milk and fresh strawberries on my cereal.

Later at our school Mass, I again renewed my heartfelt prayers that the hungry child would have something to eat.

Time came for communion. I approached the altar, as is custom, with hands outstretched. Suddenly an unexpected awareness gripped me—this was the same gesture the starving child offered as a plea. But there was a difference: I was asking for the Bread of Life, and she was begging for bread to live.

I realized that I had been praying as the disciples did in the Gospel of Luke. The worn-out crowd of five thousand was hungry, and the disciples of Jesus begged him to give the crowd something to eat.

Jesus replied with these words, "Give them some food yourselves," as the Gospel of Luke records in 6:13 (NAB).

With Jesus' words, an unwanted and forbidding sense of God's issuing a demanding call crashed upon me. I began desperately to beg God to ask anything of me, but not for my physical presence in the desert of Sudan. Yet, I also knew in my heart that fidelity to my vocation required me to consider preparing my passport, getting the necessary vaccinations, and packing my bags. So I began, slowly and hesitantly.

These preparations brought home the reality of my upcoming departure for Sudan. Inwardly I felt riddled with doubts and uncertainties. At times I was overcome by fear. Was I really being called to feed starving children on another continent? Did I have the courage it would take? How would I handle my own hunger, the desert heat, and the inevitable malaria?

I had more questions than answers as I closed my carefully arranged suitcase and wished I could pack away my insecurities and fears as neatly.

Within three months, I would arrive at Wad El Hileau, the smallest of the thirty-five camps spread throughout northern

Sudan. It was home to twelve thousand starving Sudanese and Ethiopians. Nothing could have prepared me for what I saw. Hundreds of tents were sprawled across a dry, barren desert. With the absence of latrines, human waste was scattered everywhere. Children, emaciated with starvation, sat listlessly in the dust. Mothers with shriveled breasts were sitting alongside them, trying to feed their infants. Too weak to interact, the mothers' and children's silence was caught up in the swooshing and howling of the hot afternoon sandstorms.

The enormity of the situation overwhelmed me and a debilitating depression rendered me immobile. For two days I lay collapsed on a simple construction of poles and rope that we relief workers called a bed, mentally plotting how I could return home. I had responded by coming, but could not endure staying.

I do not remember the exact moment it happened. Into my thatched hut strode one of the refugee camp doctors, gaunt with several months of dedicated service. She gazed tenderly at me and then offered a knowing smile.

"How have you done it this long?" I quietly asked, with a heart overwhelmed with sadness.

Sighing from deep within, she revealed the mystery of her being able to cope and to minister day after day. She stared directly into my fear-filled eyes and depressed heart.

"I carefully feed the child in front of me and I don't think about the hundreds who are still hungry. One-on-one is how it's done," she said, quoting Mother Teresa of Calcutta.

The words reverberated in my heart, much like a mantra, encouraging and strengthening me. They fortified my spirit and brought me courage.

"One-on-one is how it's done," I whispered to myself as I rose up, fending off my paralysis and depression with these loving words.

Day after day for a year, I trekked across the barren and hot desert to the feeding center of straw mats and makeshift overhangs. Day after day, I handed a bowl of hot milk or corn porridge, one-on-one.

To be with starving and dying children every day is anguished misery. Gathering wood for the fire, worrying about having enough water to mix with the powdered milk, waiting hours for the milk to boil, walking across a desert in unbearable heat six times a day to feed hungry stomachs, wondering how many children would die—this was too much for me to endure.

One can be tempted to stop feeding the starving; to ignore the tears and stoically bury the dead—to surrender to drought and famine taking its natural course. Heartbreakingly, one can become comfortable with misery. Something happens within that prevents famine from continuing to shock or to jolt. A relief worker can slip into looking upon intense deprivation, starvation, and suffering as normal and ordinary.

Over and over during that time, I prayed for the inward grace to keep compassion alive, the fires of tender care burning, and the passion within me to alleviate the sufferings of children. With that prayer I asked myself, *Where could that grace be found?*

As I watched a doctor from Chicago, on leave from a flourishing practice, cry with an Ethiopian mother as her child lay dying of malaria, my prayer was answered.

And my prayer was answered when I found strength in the smile of a bone-thin Sudanese mother as she wrapped her newborn in clean rags and lifted him high to Allah in praise and thanksgiving.

And my prayer was answered when Berhana's eyes lit up as I handed her the bowl of milk and she kissed my hand. I knew I could continue to feed her, and feed others.

One-on-one is how it's done.

MINING OUR FAITH, ENRICHING OUR LIFE

When have I experienced being stretched beyond my physical or mental limits? What painful or overwhelming situation now challenges me to handle it one step at a time?

———•—•—•———

SHORT PAUSE *Chain Reaction*

As adults, we tend to see life as a series of sporadic events that have little or no connection. We check days off the calendar, one at a time. In a word, we snip life into little pieces.

So, isn't it charming when children avoid this dissection and simply remind us to live beyond a piecemeal life? Having little interest in timelines, they experience life as one great weaving.

That was my first-grade student Dominic's view: "Wow! My brother was born on December 7. My granny was born on December 8. And my dad was born on December 9. Boy, talk about a chain reaction."

When I heard Dominic say this, I thought: *We adults need to take out a loom.* Weaving together more present moments and a few chain reactions could make for a lovely life tapestry!

———•—•—•———

SHORT PAUSE *Lots in Common*

"What's a nun?" my Appalachian neighbor Sally asked over beans and cornbread.

"A nun is someone who makes three promises. We promise to live simply and share our money. We love the whole world as family, and we seek God's will every day."

"Miss Bridget, me and Lloyd, that's how we live. We share our money; we love everybody up the creek; we live every minute as it comes."

Then, clanking her spoon on the table, Sally blurted: "Hain't it wonderful? You bein' a church lady and me bein' a hillbilly, and we got so much in common."

To this day, I sometimes wonder if Sally "gets" it better than most of us: the fact is there is so much more that unites us than divides us.

Reading Clouds

ON ATTENTION TO LEARNING

What can the book of life teach me
about living with attention to my senses?

Ida Jean calls Dog Lick Hollow in the hills of Appalachia her home. She lives in a three-room house with her mother, seven brothers and sisters, and a host of stray animals taken in because they needed a home.

I first met Ida Jean when she repeated third grade. She sat shyly in the back of the room with little reason to look up. Her school records contained a single sentence of evaluation: "She hain't learned nothin'."

This was far from true. She could call trees by name and she knew when a "growin' shower" was coming by the feel of the wind on her face. She anticipated when tango gut would bloom in the hills and would gather it before it was gone. Ida Jean could smell a copperhead before she glimpsed it and also could tend a fire. She knew to plant potatoes in the dark of the moon and to cut her hair in the last quarter.

Indeed, Mother Earth was her teacher. Ida Jean watched her every move, learned from her, and confided in her as one confides in an imaginary friend.

Ida Jean did learn to read and do math. She learned to tell time even as she lives in the present. She learned self-esteem as she taught others the skill of reading clouds.

One day, she proclaimed with a "spring shower" of pride, "Reckon when I'm growed, I'll be a teacher."

What Ida Jean did not realize was that she had already become a teacher. She challenged me to pack up and put aside my school bag of academic evaluations, growth charts, and personal criteria for what a successful education meant. Her lessons taught me what parents and teachers often forget: a large part of education occurs after 3:00 PM.

———•+•+•———

MINING OUR FAITH, ENRICHING OUR LIFE

What lessons do I need to learn about true education? Who are my teachers and what "study guides" do I have?

SHORT PAUSE *Bluebirds and Baobabs*

Ten-year-old Fatou lived in the bush of Senegal, West Africa, where life was a continuously raw struggle. I would watch Fatou walk long distances either to gather water at the only village well or to search for firewood. She would return gracefully and at ease with her bucket or bundle balanced on her head. Sometimes I would hear her singing as she strolled along or would observe her admiring finch-sized bluebirds in the oddest of places.

One evening, when the moon was full, Fatou invited me to catch a glimpse of the nightly white bloom of the baobab tree. She told me to bring a piece of charcoal in my pocket for protection; to tread softly for safety; and to whisper for security. "Little naughty spirits," she said, "live under the baobab, close to the roots. They get upset easily." I never discovered the source of these beliefs she held. But I fully admired the exquisite baobab flower and tasted its fruit the next morning.

Even the soggy rainy season delighted Fatou. With mud oozing between her toes she would revel in a downpour and would twirl and dance in the refreshing rain. Throwing back her head, she would open wide her mouth and drink from heaven's well.

Knowing Fatou prodded me to ask myself why I often trudge through a day's demanding schedule, oblivious to the signs of

life around me. Why do I spend so much time bemoaning the
monotony of daily routine? Through her actions, Fatou reminded
me that life is for singing and dancing in the rain, sharing playful
moments, and savoring luscious fruit. Fatou taught me that life
is not meant to be simply endured, but life is meant to be lived
fully, in attendance to the littlest detail.

Light and Vision

ON ATTENTION TO WONDER

How does delight in the wonder of the present moment
mysteriously join heaven and earth?

On November 13, 1909, the vast Nebraska sky bent down, enfolded the premature newborn into its arms, and welcomed Eveline Elizabeth McNeal into the world. In its embrace, the azure heavens pledged to shape her vision and fill her with light.

As a child, Eveline learned, through confusing experiences, that she didn't see what others saw, nor did she see objects in the same way. She had to turn her head completely to see things on either side, a habit others, unaware of her lack of peripheral vision, often noticed. Eveline didn't realize that this visual challenge would affect how she saw the world and would also be the way she would sharpen her perception of life.

On summer nights, with strains of her father's fiddling and her mother's piano drifting into the cool air, Eveline would sit peacefully on her porch. This gangly tomboy would gaze at the stars for hours and, in between reciting snatches of poetry, she would muse about the infinity of the sky. She thought it glanced back, and she reveled as she sensed its nurturing care.

As the years went on, Eveline took another look at her life. Under the night sky, she envisioned comets, cumulus clouds, celestial bodies, classrooms, and children. She dreamed about becoming a teacher and a nun.

In 1930, heaven issued her call. Eveline Elizabeth entered the religious order of Ursuline nuns and became Sister Mary Xavier of the Immaculate Heart. Thus began her love story with God and with each child she taught. Her habit of looking at things from the left and the right became her secret to compassion, understanding, and acceptance both in the chapel and in the classroom. This physical habit had taught her heart to see God, life, and children from all angles.

I met "Mary Xav," as we nuns affectionately called her, in the late 1970s, when she was assigned to our religious community in Illinois. She was in frail health, as a result of a stroke at the age of fifty-two, and had to deal with constant fatigue and hoarseness. Nevertheless, she was a bundle of spiritual energy and strength. Her life wasn't dazzling like the Northern Lights or a falling star streaking across the sky; it was more like twinkling stars over the Nebraska cornfields. And those stars formed a constellation of homespun wisdom that illuminated my own life and gave me cause to pause. "You never make a mistake by being kind to God's people. My neighbor is God. So how could I treat anyone badly?" she would ask, while at the same time offering a lesson.

Over the years, we cultivated our friendship and spiritual companionship. Her keen awareness sharpened mine. Her hands, as though holding the holy, would cup a wildflower in reverence and fascination. I watched her clap in jubilation when she received a ten-pound bag of garden fertilizer for her birthday. Tears rolled down her face as she heard in the news about starving children, or about the homeless, or poor and abused women, and I felt her black hole of anguish. Her life was clearly touched by the heavens, but her gaze was riveted upon the earth.

When I left Illinois for Appalachia, Mary Xav, and another religious sister were the first to visit me at Sandy Lick Hollow. She eyed the beauty of the hills, thought copperheads had a right to their environs, sorted rummage, trekked up the hollows to visit our neighbors, managed the oil lamps and outhouses, and enamored my neighbor Bird. He observed her and then declared, "Right good woman you got there, Sissy. She has some kind of glow in her. Like from the stars."

"Maybe, Bird," I replied, smiling, "it's from the heavens."

"No matter, Sissy, where it done come from. It's there and it twinkles."

That weekend, the Nebraska sky stretched its promise all the way east to Appalachia.

As broad daylight gave way to the nightfall of old age, Mary Xav accepted her loss of memory and physical diminishment with surrender, peace, and chuckles. In the small ways of drying dishes, dusting tables, feeding the birds and through her constant prayers, she continued her kindness of the present moment to her neighbors and to her God.

Without fear or distress, she waited for death with the anticipation she felt for the Nebraska sunsets. "I got so excited about death today," she whispered toward the end of her life. "I was thinking about seeing my mother and father, my grandmother, grandfather, and so many friends. Then I got surprised at myself. Maybe I ought to be thinking about seeing God first." She didn't realize that she had, in fact, seen God reflected in all people and situations, life's gentle shafts of heavenly light.

"I never tire of the vastness of the skies or the wonder of so many growing things," she would repeat over and over. It was a mantra of awe, wonder, and gratitude. One time she added, "When I was praying this morning, I told God what a beautiful world he had made. Then I heard God say in my heart, 'You haven't seen anything yet.'"

On February 12, 2002, the Nebraska sky bent down again, enfolded this woman of light and vision into its arms, and welcomed her home. Sister Mary Xavier of the Immaculate Heart saw her God face-to-face. God, who had been with her in all the seasons of her life and who had come to her in every child and neighbor—this God she loved so much, in turn, showed her everything.

———•———

MINING OUR FAITH, ENRICHING OUR LIFE
How might a sense of wonder foster contemplation and silence in my life? In what practical ways might I tap into the senses that I often overlook?

———•———

SHORT PAUSE *Mysterious Time*

How time flies! We try to capture it in photographs or measure it with Rolex watches and atomic clocks. Yet, mysterious and elusive, one second gives way to the next. And we ask: *Where has all the time gone?*

"You've been here a long time, Sister," said Darlene, a resident at The Boston Home in Massachusetts, a long-term care facility for adults living with multiple sclerosis and other degenerative neurological diseases. Darlene's remark surprised me because multiple sclerosis had destroyed her sense of chronology.

"How I know is because when you first came here, I could move ten fingers. Now I can only move two."

I had to catch my breath. I had never measured time in finger mobility.

Fleeting time is always eluding our grasp, challenging us to bask in the present moment, and calling us to make the most of it.

———•••——

SHORT PAUSE *Lady with a Smile*

Second-grader Benny had come with his class to sing spooky Halloween songs at The Boston Home in Massachusetts, a long-term care facility for adults living with chronic neurological diseases.

After the performance, the little "skeleton" sidled up to Melinda, who began to type on her wheelchair talking board. It was a slow process as she had mobility in only one finger. Eight-year-old Benny patiently waited.

When she finished, Melinda pushed the button and out came the robotic voice: "You did great!" She flashed her trademark smile.

Benny gave a thumbs-up, and hugged her. "Lady, don't you worry you can't talk. You smile real good."

When we accept and love people as they are, the present moment is always filled with wonder. I realized that, that day a skeleton met a lady with a real good smile.

Bus Tickets and Ladders

*How might I discover that the best place to be
is where I am at this moment?*

She is as regal as the Hebrew queen whose name she bears.
Esther begins each business day at the ticket counter with
her meticulous method of organizing the sales counter with
precision and dignity. She shuffles and reshuffles the plastic
schedule holders until the arrangement pleases her sense of
order. She checks the clock for accuracy and wipes the phone
until it sparkles.

Those who observe her unchanging routine wait with a
curiosity seasoned with patience. Experience has taught them
that no transaction will begin before the designated time of
7:30 AM. Newcomers, however, shift from one foot to another,
nervously fingering money and glancing repeatedly at the clock.
They are on edge, restlessly wondering whether they will make
the necessary bus connections.

Oblivious that she holds the royal court at bay, Esther
continues her preparations, slowly and stately. After blowing on
the counter for the last vestige of dust and tapping her personal

code into the computer, she ceremoniously flips the OPEN sign. Customer sighs release the tension. With a satisfied smile, she proclaims her reign: "First in line, please." People move forward as Esther issues the first bus ticket of the day.

After the payment is received and the ticket passed across the counter, another transaction occurs. Esther stretches her arms high, spreads her fingers wide, sways slightly, and proclaims, "May you be blessed and thank you, Jesus." Old-timers graciously respond; newcomers embarrassingly stare. One learns over time that with your bus ticket comes a free voucher for life's journey. Whether it is a piece of simple advice—"Bus to Maine runs better with coffee"—or solid reflection—"God's got every minute worked out for you"—Esther has her counsel measured by the length of the customer line and her intuition of your personal need.

One dreary winter day, an unsuspecting customer sauntered up to buy a ticket. I listened from the middle of the line, eager to hear the preaching of the day. I sensed from the look on Esther's face that she had an important message to promulgate. Holding the purchased ticket loosely in her hand, but not ready to let go of it, she leaned as far over the counter as she comfortably could. "Blessed be the Lord," she began. "Need to tell you something. Some people spend all their energy climbing the rungs of life's ladder." Peering directly at the surprised traveler and then leaning back with her signal laugh, she continued, "Then one day they discover they got their ladder against the wrong wall. Better lean on Jesus or nothing at all." Beaming with a preacher's satisfaction, she handed over the bus ticket. No one applauded, but my heart cried *Amen!*

Esther has made this Massachusetts bus station her congregation. No one escapes her gentle notice, especially those labeled and regarded as vagrants. Over the months, a homeless woman had taken a prominent place in the bus station and in the eyes of onlookers. She would spend time packing and unpacking her suitcase, looking at each garment as though it had a story to tell. Then she would fold it carefully and replace it in its reserved space in her case.

But it was her hair that caused public consternation. Raised twelve inches above her head, her hair was adorned with several decorative silk scarves tied together to meet under her chin. She would spend time in the ladies' room combing it and primping in front of the mirror, unaware that others were mirroring her actions in mockery. It appeared to some to be a "rat's nest" with its own bed of lice, but to her it was her crown of glory.

I decided to ask Esther about this woman, so I lingered at the ticket counter until everyone else had been served. Gingerly, I approached. "Esther," I said, "you know the woman with the hair. . . ."

Esther interrupted me immediately. Extending her hands in a gesture of acceptance, she stated with imposing solemnity, "That is Miss Jolene Jackson. *Miss* Jolene Jackson." Then she continued, "She packs and unpacks with nowhere to go and no one to talk to. She only has us. We don't know all she's been through in life, but I'm betting you, it's been tough. So it is best to look on her with love or not look at all." With a "praise God" on her lips, Esther resumed selling tickets.

I returned to the bus lobby. There she was: Miss Jolene Jackson. I repeated her name over and over in my heart. Suddenly, I no longer saw her as a homeless vagrant with an exaggerated head of hair or a victim of a compulsive disorder. I saw her as a Southern belle, sitting on a veranda sipping lemonade on a sultry July afternoon. She was engaged in the news of the day as she fanned herself in the summer heat. She was *Miss* Jolene Jackson.

Esther does not smother people with sharp judgments or wall them into spaces that do not fit them. She knows what inner spaciousness is. She refuses to list those who do not fit the norm into the categories society has constructed for them.

As she sells bus tickets with noble serenity, she can praise God loud and clear within the hearing of startled and harried commuters. She can laugh with those who appear as court jesters and counsel those who think themselves royal philosophers. Esther's eyes are wide open for southern belles and spirit-hungry

travelers in a bus station. She knows who needs a surprise
voucher and who lugs extra baggage—all because she surveys
her kingdom from the heights of a ladder that leans on Jesus.

———

MINING OUR FAITH, ENRICHING OUR LIFE
  *What new spiritual landscape would I like to explore? What extra baggage
  might I courageously leave behind?*

———

SHORT PAUSE *Another Story*

  In his youth, Father Murphy was a blacksmith. He used to say,
"Time spent over a fire has forged a nine-hundred-year-old secret
of holiness in my heart." With a leprechaun wink, he added, "If
this secret is heeded, we will all become saints."

> To live above
> With the saints we love—
> Oh! What glory.
>
> But to live below
> With the folks we know—
> That's another story!

With our eyes fixed upon the heavens, we dream about the lives of the saints and pray to emulate their virtues. We may forget that they had to live, like us, with the folks below, in the present moment—in moments of folly and in moments of glory. It was precisely this that made them holy, a conviction hammered into Father Murphy's heart.

———•••———

SHORT PAUSE *Autumn Leaves*

People were opening windows, slipping off jackets and sweaters, and growing restless. Autumn's nip had given way to an unusually hot, Indian summer day. Even the temperatures of the thirty-seven irritated passengers in the small, jam-packed local bus were rising.

Neither the city traffic nor the signals cooperated. Some traffic lights were flashing yellow due to street repairs and others turned red as soon as our bus approached. The ruts and bumps of the broken road jarred our backs. As a group of passengers, we were getting angry.

Suddenly, the bus driver, a thirty-something, burly fellow, stopped the bus near a maple tree that was ablaze in autumnal glory. Sensing a mechanical problem, the agitated passengers let out a collective sigh and some language as colorful as the fall season.

Unexpectedly, the music of the old song "Autumn Leaves" filled the bus. Our bus driver was playing a harmonica with rhythm and sway. Surprise turned to laughter as we began clapping and humming along.

Our accompaniment was interrupted as our transit musician called out, "Everybody, look at that maple tree over there. It won't ever look like that again. Catch it while you can." After the final lingering trill, he slipped his harmonica back into his pocket, switched on the bus, and off we went.

The bus driver was right. Soon this maple tree's brilliance would yield to winter barrenness as its fiery red and orange leaves would begin to fall and twirl in street dancing. But to the sound of music, we had caught it in the present moment.

Popo and Tortillas

How might gentle nurturing of my family and friends become a blessing for future generations?

Josefina, who is eight, adores her parents. She knows that they are both hard working and loving. Outside of her school hours, she shadows these lights of her life.

Some days, before the rooster crows, Josefina accompanies her father and Popo, the family donkey, on milk deliveries. They walk slowly, greeting Ixtaccíhuatl and Popocatépetl, the sleeping mountains of their Mexican village.

Again and again Josefina's father recounts for her the folk tale of the forbidden love between the Toltec princess and the Chichimec prince. He tells her how the two enemy kings did not care about the dreams of their children. What Josefina cherishes most is that her father always asks her about her dreams and promises to help fulfill them.

Sometimes her father points out all the "green gold" that Cortés left behind. Reminding her that it is the most important kind, he shows her the treasure of medicinal herbs and healing plants growing along the paths.

"Look to God for health," he says, "and then look under your feet."

It is not difficult for Josefina to look to the Divine, for she thinks God is just like her father.

She looks to her mother too, whose hands fascinate her. Rough and calloused with little spots and wrinkles, they become beautiful and graceful while she is making the day's tortillas. Josefina wonders if she herself will acquire the skill of patting, flipping, and baking them just right. As she watches her mother, she can begin to smell and taste them, as they will be served warm and oozing with cheese and beans.

Her mother hums as she works. When Josefina tells her that she sings sweeter than the birds, her mother beams, her eyes radiating unconditional love. Josefina bathes in that warmth and light.

Nights are quiet and peaceful. Gathering around their home altar, the family lights the candles in honor of Our Lady of Guadalupe. With hands folded, or sometimes joined, each gives thanks and praise for the day. Together they sing a closing hymn to the glory of God and a good-night song to *La Virgencita*.

Then each child kneels for a parental blessing. Josefina feels the strength of her father and the gentleness of her mother. Her father prays for her safety and good health; her mother, for guidance and peace. After long hugs, she snuggles in her warm bed and realizes that heaven has begun.

Josefina will always be someone's child—and perhaps, one day, someone's parent who, with calloused hands, makes tortillas oozing with cheese and blesses her children with peace.

———•••———

MINING OUR FAITH, ENRICHING OUR LIFE
What hopes and dreams do I cherish for my family and for myself? What treasures of wisdom lie under my feet?

———•••———

SHORT PAUSE *Any Relation?*

Sharia was a second-grader in my learning center who struggled to master the written word. It was painful for me, her teacher, to watch her diligent attempts to decode simple words with anxious hesitation or, even worse, to no avail.

Sharia had no trouble with the spoken word: she knew just the right word to use to console a classmate; she could delightfully tell a "Knock, Knock" joke in her Irish lilt; or lead a class prayer with undistracted devotion.

Her parents' endearment bridged the gap in Sharia's academic difficulties. She was the apple of her daddy's eye and to her mother, a "honey of a peach."

One cold February day, I realized just how much this parental adulation meant to her. Bounding into the classroom and staring at me with intense earnestness, Sharia asked, "Sister, do you think my daddy could be God's baby brother?"

Taken aback, I began to frantically search and fumble for words. With an excited breath, she quickly continued, "Daddy's *soooo* good to me, and I think he learned it from God."

Sharia's exuberant statement had me asking myself, *What am I learning from God?*

PART TWO

Trusting in Divine Care

From the time I was a little child, my mother would say to me, "God will take care of you." Then she gave me a hanky, a hug, or a bidding to "go play." This assurance would dry my tears, mend bicycle scratches, and bless me as I made clover crowns in the summer grass. These words made me feel safe and secure though I wasn't quite sure *what* God's care looked like or *how* it happened.

Years later, through two important experiences, I would understand this to be the second practice of the abundant life: accepting and trusting in divine care.

The first experience was in December 1961. My mother had given my younger brothers the ultimatum: "Boys, sort your toys without hemming and hawing if you expect Santa Claus to come this year." That was enough to get their wheels in motion. Broken water guns and balsa wood airplanes, stretched-out slinkies, dart sets minus darts, split bats and deflated balls, and a year's worth of odd accumulations were hauled to the front sidewalk for refuse pick-up. The newer toys were organized "in the back," as Mama called the breakfast room.

Several hours later, my brother Philip yelled for my mother to come to the bay window. An African-American man was carefully going through the discarded toys. He would examine each one, either returning it to the pile or putting it aside. His very presence, to say nothing of his rummaging through the sidewalk collection, was an unwritten, forbidden occurrence in this all-white neighborhood.

My mother went outside, asking if she could help him. The man, hesitating in fear, choked back tears. "Christmas is comin', Miss. I'm just lookin' for some toys for Santa to bring my children. Out of work now and don't have much for extras. Just been walking this neighborhood with hopes. . . ."

My mother understood even before he had time to finish his sentence. She then did what was unheard of at the time. She invited this good father into our home, and said, "Mister, you come with me. All the good stuff's inside." Then she proceeded to bring him through the front door "to the back," and told him to take whatever he wanted.

It was a "high-ticket" collection: a log cabin set, fire engine and bulldozer trucks, stunt and spinning tops, yoyos, still-boxed model airplanes, and board games with all the pieces. Thoughtfully, he selected a gift for each one of his four children. After she encouraged him to believe that God would care for his family, Mama ushered him again to the front door. With a genuine, grateful handshake and a warm, mutual Merry Christmas wish, he slowly descended the walkway and disappeared down the block.

Moving beyond Southern society's taboos of the 60s, Mama knew "race relations" meant that we are all related.

The next moment I understood more deeply about divine care was seven years later, and another December day. After my father's suicide in October, Mama was left with thousands of dollars of debt, twelve dollars in daddy's wallet, and the support of her two youngest children. She was still immersed in the lonely darkness of grief and shock. She could not meet house payments, she needed employment, and she was aware that the holidays were around the corner.

Mama loved Christmas. In fact, she would say that "every day should be Christmas" and, much to our dismay, would begin playing Christmas carols as soon as Halloween was over. However, this year the carols had come much later, and the volume went down to a whisper. Neither tree nor presents were ever mentioned.

One afternoon, however, my youngest brother broached the subject. "Mom," Albert asked, "do you think there's gonna be Christmas this year?"

My mother hugged him tightly, "Yes, Son," she said in faith, not sight, "there will always be Christmas in this home. God will take care of us."

Weeks later, several friends dissolved suicide's prevalent stigma with holiday greetings, when they surprised Mama with a Christmas fir tree. They decorated it with the hand-blown ornaments passed down from my grandparents, and our traditional colorful bubble lights. Next to the crèche, they placed beautifully wrapped presents of board games, fire trucks with sirens and movable ladders, super deluxe yoyos, and Mama's favorite rose-scented dusting powder. Then they delicately placed a tray of sugarcoated pecans and homemade pralines on the breakfast room table. Wiping away a tear, Mama quietly murmured how grateful she was that God takes care of us. These good neighbors wished my family a blessed Christmas and slowly descended the walkway, disappearing down the block.

These two incidents fleshed out for me the second practice of the abundant life. From a father's need, a mother's grief, and the neighbors' goodness, I learned that accepting and trusting in divine care does not mean that we will never suffer tragedy and immense suffering, and that feelings are not a reliable guide in measuring our acceptance. The other thing I learned about the practice of the abundant life is that often God's loving care comes through the tenderness and risk-taking of others.

As we live in attention to the present moment, it unfolds before us. With this unfolding we acknowledge the truth of our life that is before us. But we cannot stop there. From acknowledgment we move toward acceptance. With a surrendered attitude of heart, we accept what life deals us, knowing beyond a shadow of doubt that God cares for us.

Life can be hard; situations unfair; outcomes painful. We experience trials and tribulations that will make us wonder how we can cope, or even if we can—a loss of a job that deprives us of the income to provide for our family; a violent and untimely death of a loved one; a sudden illness and subsequent dependence on others. Acceptance means that we move forward, no matter how slowly, with one foot in front of the other. It means that, as we continue to trust, when all seems lost and hopeless, we may courageously pull ourselves up by our bootstraps.

Trusting in divine care asserts that no situation is too complex for God. We continue to believe in God's providence even when we see no way out, way through, or way over. As we anticipate God's grace being there for us, right down the block or around the corner, we surrender *with trust* to all the difficulties that come our way. Whatever the weight of the cross that is put upon our shoulders, we are assured that God's grace is greater than our problem.

Trusting in divine care is not measured by our feelings. There will be times when we are tempted to wonder if God has abandoned us. We may feel nothing, neither surrender nor acceptance, only a sense of walking a dark path devoid of peace and assistance. At these times we must remember that our feelings are not accurate gauges or trustworthy guides in our spiritual life. They can mislead us and even deceive us.

When we feel abandoned *by* God, we can be encouraged to abandon ourselves *to* God's divine care. This is a way of putting our faith into action. In times of discouragement and intense need, we can hear, not as mere suggestion but as imperative, the command of Jesus, in Matthew's Gospel, to *"look at* the birds of the air" and *"consider* the lilies of the field" (6:26, 28 NRSV). The birds neither sow nor reap, and yet God feeds them. The lilies neither toil nor spin and yet they grow. How much more are we worth? God knows our needs and will provide for them. God is on our side.

Etched upon my heart in these childhood memories is that we need each other. While we can proclaim that accepting divine care is an integral part of experiencing the abundant life, this remains only talk if we do not become a "sermon in shoes" for one another. If we really believe that we are God's hands, feet, and heart upon this earth, then we will be ready to meet people's needs. Whether it is food on pantry shelves, babysitting for a stressed-out parent, peanut butter sandwiches for the soccer team, we put love into action. We can give a face to divine care, often at personal sacrifice and lack of acceptance. "Life's one thing nobody can do alone," my fifth-grade student Loretta Mary insightfully explained to me in the learning center.

A gunshot shattered my mother's world and caused it to fall apart. There were moments when she caved into unbelievable grief and pain. But family, friends, and neighbors began to help her pick up the pieces and to rebuild. They made many sacrifices on her behalf, took personal risks, and offered prayers beyond count. As she did what she could herself, she also learned to lean on God and lean on others. Neither God nor friends ever failed her. Once again, with trust and acceptance, she could proclaim to her children, despite all the odds, that "God always takes care of us."

Mighty Fine

ON ACCEPTING SIMPLE JOYS

What simple experiences in life might strengthen my trust in God's care?

C hanged my name to Bird in second grade," he explained. "There was a girl in my class called Bridie like me. Didn't like sharin' a girl's name. Plus I never knew who folks wanted, me or her. Dropped out of school in third grade and never changed my name back. Besides, Bird has a nice ring to it." I smiled, looking tenderly on the West Virginia–lined face of my esteemed Appalachian neighbor.

"While we're talkin' personal, tell you somethin' else. I heared from kin that I was born in February. Government keeps sayin' I was born on the fifteenth of April. I keep to February. What do those government people know? They weren't there to tell the tale, were they? Don't reckon it matters. Fact is, I was birthed somewhere around seventy-eight years ago and here I am." No amount of explanation could set the record straight. Bird knew who he was and loved being a mountain man.

Bird lived in the arms of Sandy Lick Hollow. He was not able to read in the literal sense, but he could feel the beat of stories in the wombs of full moons, in spring greens growing on the hills, and in stormy rain clouds. Hickory logs, copperheads, and "mighty fine kindlin' wood" all had a respected page in the book of his life. Unprotected by gadgets and comforts, Bird was schooled in the raw lessons of hardship and poverty.

He lived alone. His cherished wife had died many years ago. His two sons had also died shortly after their mother. Bird never shared details of whether death had come through accident or disease; he would simply remark, "They done gone. That's the whole story." He talked about death as directly and simply as he talked about the details of his birth.

I would watch him as he sat for long stretches, a mysterious blend of monk, mystic, and Appalachian preacher. Cherishing a spot across the creek where the hills seemed to dip into the running stream, he would get a chew of tobacco and "study on things," all the while staring fixedly at the azure sky.

I wondered if he was ever lonely. One day I decided to broach the question directly, hoping that it was not a personal intrusion. "Bird, are you ever lonesome?" I asked.

He looked at me in a disbelief mixed with startled surprise. As he thought before responding, I waited, rather sure I would regret asking.

Spitting his tobacco as far as his talent allowed, he smiled rather sheepishly at me. "Sissy, you being a church lady asking me that." After taking a long pause, and repeatedly shaking his head in consternation, he continued. "When a man has a stout chair set in the shade of the pines, a good chew of *bakker*, hears the wind between heaven and earth, and knows that God is always on his side, how could he ever, ever be lonely? Lots of things hard about life in these hills, Sissy, but loneliness hain't one of them."

As we sat in the ensuing silence, Bird's words echoed deep down into the dark empty cavern of my heart. How little I knew about authentic solitude.

Bird's bravery could be the gossip of the hollow. Once he had ventured out in the midst of a violent electrical storm replete with ground lightning to tie up the pole beans. Barehanded, he coaxed a copperhead, hiding in a dank corner of the wood box, to slither out in front of his loaded pistol. And, mild mannered as he was, he had no hesitation in confronting injustice or social wrongs, whether they be poorly paid debts or family struggles about "wayward young'uns."

Yet, in spite of his courage, Bird did have *one* fear: my eternal salvation. With his indomitable spirit, he would come pleading, "Sissy, there's a revival tonight down by the river. C'mon, give your hand at the altar and go down in the waters. Then you will be saved, and my worries 'bout you will be done gone. You a good woman but you hain't got it all."

"Bird," I would patiently reply for the countless time, "I have been baptized. I have been saved. Why give only my hand when I have given my life to God?"

Then he would explain, as though for the first time. "You were still drinking your mother's milk when the water touched your forehead. And that's all it got to. You never got that blessed water in your pores, through your skin. It rolled off your head but never got through to your veins. You got to feel the water inside you. Then you *really* will be baptized and saved. It hain't never too late to three times plunge."

I never did go down to the river. But many a time, as the symphony of our creek harmonized with the still night air, I was immersed in thoughts of baptism, its meaning and its mission, and wondered if, as with solitude, there was much about it I did not understand.

The time came, one dry, hot summer day, to say good-bye to the hollow and to my beloved neighbor Bird. My spirit was bone dry. I was soon to leave for the bush of Senegal, West Africa. From my drought came a shower of tears as I hugged this lover of hills and creeks, now blind and frail, who had been for so long my neighbor, mentor, and cherished friend.

"What happens, Bird, if you die before I return?" I asked through my weeping.

"Now, Sissy," he gently and compassionately responded. "Don't you be a cryin' like that. I'll be put up purtty on the hill over yonder. It's a good place to rest."

He gathered his thoughts and continued, "You see this here body?" he asked as he patted his arm. "This is only the house I live in. When I go to die, I will have changed my dwelling. But one room will always be the same, the one that belonged to you." I hugged him tightly and realized how little I knew about death.

Bird did die while I was in Africa. Although I felt my soul crack open when I heard of his passing, envisioning him at peace upon a grassy knoll brought me comfort. Knowing that his spirit permeated my veins as certainly as the creek he so loved flowed through the hollow, eased my grief. As I remembered him sitting under the pines, oblivious to everything except earth and sky, I was consoled as the hills echoed his words, "One thing about life, Sissy. If you live it here, you are in God's care. If you pass on, you are near his throne. Either way, no matter what, you'll be mighty fine."

Now, years later, as I think back on my beloved Bird, I realize that not only his life, but what it had become, were just that— mighty fine.

⊷

MINING OUR FAITH, ENRICHING OUR LIFE

In what ways might sitting in the shade of the pines or listening to the wind roar between heaven and earth make my life mighty fine? How do I understand and accept authentic solitude, baptism, and death?

⊷

SHORT PAUSE *Around the Corner*

Eight-year-old Sherman had finally gotten his birthday wish: a new orange bicycle decorated with green wheel flaps. My third grader had waited months and had tried every approach with his parents, from nagging and whining to writing an entreating letter with a long list of promised chores.

There was one problem: Sherman did not know how to ride his bike. His every attempt resulted in tipsy slants that quickly became falls. Since he lived three houses from the school, I would watch his after-school attempts from my classroom window, silently cheering him on or wincing with his mother when he fell.

One April afternoon, Sherman seemed to have aced the method. With newfound bravery and his own brand of supersonic speed, he was pedaling down the block toward the tree-lined corner. His beaming mother stood confidently on the sidewalk.

All of a sudden, Sherman screeched to a halt and jumped off his bike. Yelling to his mother, he explained his hesitation, "It's hard to keep going when you don't know what's coming."

Sherman's excuse got me thinking about life and the future. Life has so many unknowns, twists, and turns. We never know what's coming, that's for sure. Can we believe that grace and divine care will always be just around the corner?

Serpent Handling

In what ways might an experience of another's religious devotion strengthen my own faith?

Although it was an offer that was hard to refuse, I wasn't sure I should accept. As the week passed, I continued to weigh the pros and cons of Sally's invitation.

"We'll be wantin' your answer right soon," my Appalachian friend said encouragingly. "Truck needs gassin' and clothes gotta get pressed 'fore next Wednesday night." With a perceptive inkling, she asked, "Not 'fraid, are you? If you are, don't trouble your mind. Preacher Nevins Ellis will take you right in."

That's what worried me. Several congregations had already invited me, "the church lady" as I was called, to join them in shared prayer and worship. In welcoming me as a sister and friend, these folks from the hollows had put aside their doubts and even their suspicion of Catholics' "superstitious" practices. I felt as at home in these small churches as I felt in these West Virginia hills.

But it was different with this *Jesus* church in the secluded backwoods, twenty-five miles away. I didn't want this fiery preacher, by any manner or means, to "take me right in" because Preacher Nevins Ellis and his congregation were serpent handlers.

The next day, with Appalachian protocol, Sally good-naturedly continued her urging. "You know, some people, they decide 'fore they learn. Don't seem quite fair to the folks concerned. Reckon you not one of those, are you?" Sally knew how to circle the target before hitting the bull's-eye.

Wednesday night came. Sally and I squeezed into the truck's cab while Lloyd, her husband, took the grease-laden wheel. Braving ruts, mud holes, and fallen logs, we made our way to the small clapboard church deep in the hills. Its secluded spot unnerved me, but the light of the full moon surprisingly soothed my fears. As I stood in its glow and clasped my friend's hand, I sensed that the "why" of worship is so much more important than the "how."

Inside, the church was devoid of any religious paintings. There was neither sanctuary nor choir loft. Only the word *Jesus* was painted in bold red letters in their places.

With eyes riveted on the crucifix that hung around my neck, Preacher Nevins Ellis greeted us, "We don't take kindly to graven images." Clearly receiving the message, I slipped my cross off and into my pocket. The preacher nodded graciously and extended his hand. With the finest of hospitality, we were shown to our seats and asked to reverently await the arrival of the "holy boxes."

Within a few moments, a hymn began. It was something about God loving us even when the moon becomes blood. Sally turned to me and whispered, "You know that will never happen while we live. But God's love happens every day we live." I began to feel the depth of faith that united this small congregation.

With a ritualistic procession the boxes were brought into the church. "The serpents have come, fresh and clean from their bathing." Sally must have glimpsed my astonished look as she explained, "Reckon you would never have the wine in dirty cups, would you?" I shook my head.

Preacher Nevins called the assembly to worship with an introduction of his "honored guests who traveled far in the moon's light and the hollow's dirt to come." Then he declared, "My sisters and brothers, they have done brought us a message. Let us listen to our sister Bridget, who is not of our faith but of our God."

My heart skipped like a stone across the creek as I realized I was being asked to "declare unto the others the word God had given me from the Bible to cry out." I felt unprepared on two counts. My voice was waning in sheer nervousness, and my hands were empty. I was the only one there who did not have a Bible.

Mustering my memory and trusting that John's Gospel, chapter fourteen, would not disappoint, I began the words of assurance and comfort. "Let not your hearts be troubled. Believe in God; believe. . . ."

I had barely uttered this verse when Preacher Nevins interrupted with loud shouts of affirmation. He began to dance and twirl in a circle, occasionally pausing in the rhythm to jump from side to side and click his heels. He then began his sermon in a singsong voice, basing each part on the Scripture passage I had chosen. Sally's words echoed in my heart. He did, indeed, "take me right in."

After about two hours of shouting "Amen," singing, clapping, and swaying in our pews, Preacher Nevins asked the anointed to come forth. Several people approached him and opened the tightly shut boxes. Reverend Nevins removed several serpents and handed them over to those who felt called by the Almighty.

We began singing again. This led to intense twirling dances of ecstatic devotion. It was as though the handlers had lost any concept of time or space as they spun free-style, swayed with passion, and reverently pirouetted. The serpents twisted around necks, rolled down backs and chests, and were fondled in hands and on arms. It was complete surrender in faith to the claim of Jesus in Mark's Gospel that reads, "They will pick up serpents in my name."

These mountain people had picked up serpents in God's name. But they had gone one step further. They professed their belief that they had been anointed and chosen to do so, accepting this call in faith and surrender.

In the early hours of Thursday morning, the service ended. The group of thirty-five filed out, stopping briefly at a framed photo. It was a picture of the former pastor in his coffin, dead from a serpent bite. People paused, nodded, and solemnly went on their way.

Preacher Nevins was waiting for us. "Sister," he said, "I am urged to speak some words. We know that God keeps his promise. That's why we are serpent handlers. I sure appreciate when people call us that and not snake handlers. Snakes are sly; serpents are in the Bible.

"Anyway, the best death possible is being serpent-bit 'cuz you go out trusting his word. Sometimes you die for the rest of us. We all got to live moving forward. But sometimes we backslide and God comes, in one way or another, to remind us."

He reverently touched the picture and continued, "Our last pastor, quite a man he was. Never took nothing, not even aspirin, when that serpent bit. We gathered and prayed, and we tried to comfort him in his suffering. Not every bite leads to death. But his did. Reckon, as head of our church, there were some not living up to what the people promised God. So maybe

God didn't live up to what he promised us. It's a two-way street sometimes in life."

Then, with tenderness and understanding, Preacher Nevins took my hand. With a slight bow of blessing and looking me straight in the eye, he peered beyond the crucifix in my pocket and into my heart, saying, "Watch your backslidin' and pray real steady to go out believin'."

***

MINING OUR FAITH, ENRICHING OUR LIFE

In what ways do I compromise or backslide in matters of faith or practice? What personal prejudices inhibit my appreciation of different religious rituals and beliefs?

***

SHORT PAUSE *Love's Measure*

A Boston talk show host was organizing a fundraiser for a young man, paralyzed two years before by a gunshot. The radio host reminded us that, although we may have forgotten the incident, this young fellow still needed our generous support.

These words brought me back to my experience in the desert of Sudan. Although I had promised myself that I would never forget the misery there, I had, over time, unconsciously put those memories on life's back burner.

I recalled how, months after returning from the refugee camp, a relief worker had sent me a little slip of paper. It contained a message from Gebre, an Ethiopian teenager. "I am still here," the note said. "Do you remember what life is like for me?" Much to my personal chagrin, I had to stop and recall life in the East African desert. Indeed, it was so easy to forget circumstances in the refugee camp as life, USA-side, went on.

The talk show host was right: the measure of love and compassion is how long we remember.

———

SHORT PAUSE *Rising Waters*

It was August of 2007. Against the backdrop of the still-cresting Ohio floodwaters, a middle-aged woman stood before a pile of rubble and debris, once her home with its safely guarded and treasured possessions. As she realized the extent of her loss, the terror in her eyes overpowered her words.

Reverently and compassionately, the news interviewer asked her, "What will you do now?"

After a long pause, she responded from a well deep inside her. With a courage tempered with reality and drawn from faith, the woman responded, "I'll start with what I got left and, with God's grace, go on."

In our "going on," divine waters well up and push us forward.

Desert-Baked Tears

ON ACCEPTING COMPASSION

How might my personal acts of compassion
become God's way of providing for the needs of others?

Sulemon, one of the 12,500 Ethiopians in the refugee camp of Wadi Hileau, Sudan, East Africa, proved to be a trustworthy friend. He was a starving child: the victim of the ravages of the famine. I knew that he would survive when the day came that he had the strength to take the bowl of hot milk from my hands and sip it himself. He kept growing stronger and, at nine years of age, became my interpreter as we went from tent to tent looking for malnourished children to bring to the feeding center. Sulemon could speak Amharic, Arabic, and a few words of English.

But it was his big, black eyes that communicated what I needed most to know. With a single glance they could speak out the secrets and desires of those he called family. As we met with others, his eyes would also write the day's homework in big black letters on the chalkboard of my heart: "Bring an extra high-energy biscuit." "Smile and give her hope." "Let him know that tomorrow we will come again."

Every day, Sulemon would join six hundred other children for daily rations of corn porridge and hot milk. I still remember the day he began a chant of thanks to Allah as the large buckets of milk came into the feeding center. This starving child did not yet realize his basic human right to food; but he did know that Allah feeds the hungry.

One day he exclaimed: "You teach!" and with that, he changed the lives of the children.

Sulemon's bidding sparked the teacher within me. We would wait for the gray rats to eat the crumbs from the Oxfam high-energy biscuits and lick the milk that lingered on the feeding mats. Then children would gather and classes began. Simple things, such as lessons in hygiene and a little English, caught their attention.

Then, when Sulemon put on a sack stamped "Powdered Milk, Gift of the United States of America," took an empty plastic box from the Oxfam biscuits, and began to beat his drum, music returned to the lives of the children. His eyes—and theirs—conveyed an enthusiasm and strength amid the tragedies of a drought and a civil war.

On a dark, windy morning, I was to leave Sudan to return to the United States. My faithful friend stood in the distance, his desperate tears baked by a morning heat. When Sulemon saw me in the truck, he came running to say good-bye. We both knew we would never see each other again. He touched the sky with his hands and then touched my eyes. Through the pool of shared tears, the message was spoken without a word: "When I meet Allah and you meet God, let us ask about each other."

From this land of plenty, I think of Sulemon, his life unchanged in a land of want. I recall the secrets in his big, black eyes; hear the echo of his chants of gratitude; watch him dancing in a powdered milk sack; and feel his desert-baked tears. As I struggle with my own complacency and consumerism, I remember our promise to ask God about each other and often wonder how he is.

———•◦•———

MINING OUR FAITH, ENRICHING OUR LIFE

In what ways do my complacency and consumerism affect the global community? What positive actions might I take to balance the inequities in our world?

SHORT PAUSE *Sweater Tag*

Five-year-old Cias was slowly dying in our Sudan feeding center.

One day after receiving a shipment of knitted sweaters from a British senior citizens' group, I selected red, purple, and yellow sweaters for Cias. He would enjoy choosing his color.

He beamed as he stretched out his skeleton-like hand for the yellow one. I noticed a small tag pinned to the sleeve. The handwriting was shaky but the message was clear: "I made this for you because I care about you. I hope you have food. God bless you, little child. Love from the U.K."

When it comes to compassionate caring, distance never matters. Love's embracing arms always stretch far enough.

SHORT PAUSE *Searching for Words*

As I hid under my bedcovers, my feelings of inadequacy caused me to toss and turn for three nights. Here I was, a writer, primary reading specialist, and language arts teacher, at a loss for words. Jacqui was returning to my first grade after a week's absence, and I simply did not know what to say to her.

Her six-month-old brother, Brian Patrick, rosy-cheeked with green-hills-of-Ireland eyes, had died of sudden infant death syndrome. Jacqui, who spent every extra moment with him, needed my words of comfort. She was too young to read the grief in my heart.

As soon as she appeared at our classroom door, her friend Michelle jumped out of her chair and dashed to hug her. "Jacqui," she said, "I know you are really, *really* sad 'cuz baby Brian died. He didn't even get to walk or talk. But you know what? Now he gets to grow up with God."

A six-year-old had unearthed her teacher's buried words.

Nothing Too Small

ON ACCEPTING DEPENDENCE

*In what ways might my own dependence on others call forth
the marvels of divine care?*

Julia, a three-year-old, was dying of AIDS. Each day, dressed
in a new outfit—perhaps her mother's way of covering a sense
of guilt—she arrived at the HIV/AIDS day care. Deaf, blind, and
epileptic, Julia lived in a dark, silent world of seizures and pain.
Her arms and legs flailed constantly as she tried to determine the
boundaries of her external space.

We would carry her to the toddlers' room and begin another
day of total care and therapy. The other toddlers cuddled
and hugged her in unconditional acceptance and joy at her
presence.

After two years, her daily care became a challenge. The
little improvement and even small victories, such as sitting
unsupported for a minute or two, failed to satisfy our need for
major results. We wondered what her life was all about and
what our role was in it. The demands of her medical conditions
were exhausting, and we seemed fixed in a no-win, no-payback
situation. Our unspoken thoughts spoke volumes.

Julia died on Thanksgiving Day. As families celebrated with feast and festive gatherings, Julia's mother sat alone, a single mother without family, enduring the loss of her only child and the pain of years of addiction.

As we grieved Julia's absence, we began to reflect on the meaning of a life so fragile and short. We recalled the days it was difficult to continue our own self-giving love with its desire for rewards and compensations.

We shared simple memories: how peacefully she slept; how she relished yogurt taste by taste; how her physical aversion to touch slowly disappeared; how vital she was to our work at the day care; how empty the days now seemed without her.

In these moments we came to understand that she bestowed a gift on us that no other child ever had. In her very dependence, she gave us, who were growing weak in our loving, the strength to continue each day. She reminded us that love can still be love, even when it is devoid of feeling or craves recompense.

In remembering Julia, we realized we needed her. Her physical weakness had become our inner strength. She had opened our blind eyes and deaf ears to the challenge of unconditional love. We came to believe that, even in the midst of doubt and painful questions, no act of love can be measured—nor is it ever wasted.

MINING OUR FAITH, ENRICHING OUR LIFE

In what ways might the power of daily and seemingly monotonous acts of love change my life and the lives of others? What spiritual aids might I depend on to avoid growing tired of doing good?

SHORT PAUSE *Locusts*

After three years of drought, rain came to Lehar, West Africa, and the millet harvest would be abundant. There was rejoicing in the village!

But one morning, I heard people screaming across the bush: "Locusts, locusts are coming!" Within ten minutes, the entire millet crop was gone. Nothing remained to be harvested.

Everything within me cried out, "Why?" Certainly, of all people, the poor should be the first to be cared for. Yet, hunger would again be rampant.

Once again, I asked the ancient question: *God, how could you allow this to happen? Is this how you treat your children?*

As I was busy interrogating God, the villagers were planning the next planting season, mapping out fields, and discussing shared tools. Experiencing their contagious confidence, my theological questions slowly melted, dissolving into the villagers' trust in divine care and in their hope for a future harvest.

—•◦•—

SHORT PAUSE *The Yellow Line*

For years, Dennis drove a "semi" for a large grocery store chain. "I could handle that rig through ice, blinding rain, snow-storms, and just plain bumper-to-bumper traffic. I reveled in every minute on the road," he told me one September day.

Now Dennis, a strapping man in his fifties, is living with multiple sclerosis in a Massachusetts long-term care facility. "My biggest challenge was to learn and practice the 'sip and blow' method of using a straw to move my wheelchair. I finally succeeded and got my wheelchair to the elevator. But guess what happened then? Nobody was around to push the button." Dennis chuckled.

"I've also learned how to manage," he continued. "I've decided to live each day on a positive note. When I wake up, I tell myself it's going to be a good day. After all, I can still move my head and speak. Attitude's everything and opens the door to acceptance."

"Plus," he reflected, "I think about this story my mother taught me years ago. I don't know if it's true, but they say that on each barge that moves along the Thames in England, there's a yellow line painted down the center. When the cargo is balanced and is in proportion to the weight of the barge, the yellow line is clearly visible. This is what each person manning the docks looks for—the yellow line. If it can't be seen, then it's time to shift the load, reduce it, or hand it over to another barge."

Pausing to take a deep breath and slowly sip from his water bottle, Dennis mused, "You see, life's like that. We all have something to carry. Each morning, I see God looking at my yellow line, and I know that he promises to keep his eye on it. Trusting that, I know that my barge can bear the weight of the day."

An autumn conversation, one-lane roads, and "no passing" zones are good reminders to confidently stay the course and to courageously finish our journey.

Forgotten Birthday

ON ACCEPTING INDIFFERENCE

When my special anniversaries are forgotten or my
achievements applied to another, how might I use these
occasions to deepen my prayer and gratitude?

Nicky, a teenager of fourteen, wanted to keep his brothers and sisters together as a family. He was one of four children, each with a different father. Nicky and his siblings were homeless, city children, moving from place to place on the north side of St. Louis, Missouri. Because they were in and out of different schools, they were overlooked by the educational system and received most of their knowledge from the streets.

Nicky's mother, a drug addict, was serving eighteen months for possession. His biological father had long since disappeared. The children were placed in foster homes, separated, alone, and missing each other.

Soon after his placement, Nicky ran away from foster care. He lived on the streets and found a job working ten hours a day at a car wash. Convinced that he could persuade his father to reunite and care for the family, Nicky hoped to save enough money to find him.

On a sweltering August day, a middle-aged businessman came to the car wash, talked a little with Nicky, tipped generously, and made Nicky an offer he could not refuse.

The man agreed to pay Nicky $20,000 to shoot a drug dealer. He would even provide the gun. He explained to Nicky that money would no longer be a problem and that he and his siblings could enjoy a home and food. It seemed like an easy plan to make his dream come true.

The next week, Nicky followed instructions, sought the victim out, and pulled the trigger. He never realized that this death would be the beginning of his own.

In anticipation that he would be tried as an adult, and receive a twenty-year state prison term, he was sent to the City Detention Center before the trial.

Every child loves a birthday. Nicky's came around, but no one noticed. He wrote a touching letter and asked the detention center chaplain to deliver it. He began:

Dear God,

Today's my birthday but no one knows or even cares. You made the sky with all the stars so I know you remember you made me. Wish we could talk stuff over but this is the best I can do. Chap said you'd get this letter. I'm so alone here, God. Is this like when we die? Chap said you'd understand, but I need more than that. Can you help me, God?

Sincerely,

Nicky

The detention center chaplain, deeply moved by Nicky's simple faith, showed me his letter to God. After reading it, I asked myself, *Who cries harder: the child who suffers, or the adult who suffers with the child?*

There are children who know death before they have truly known life. Some learn about death in a feeding center; some learn about it in a prison lock-up, wondering why, in trying to better their lives, their life begins to shut down.

Whether we are reflecting before a vast desert horizon or in a narrow cell behind bars, death remains an intimidating mystery that we often flee from in terror. As we accept death with tears and regret, we are challenged to turn and face it squarely. Only then will death release its fearful grip and hope extend her comforting embrace.

———•◦•———

MINING OUR FAITH, ENRICHING OUR LIFE

How might I explain the mystery of suffering to others, especially children? What efforts do I make to reach out to those in my family and neighborhood who are forgotten and overlooked?

———•◦•———

SHORT PAUSE *Two Dollars*

It was a festive night! The Statue of Liberty was reopening in New York, and Mama and I were watching the ceremonies on TV in New Orleans. Millions of dollars had gone into this extensive renovation.

"Mama, isn't this wonderful? Listen to the music and look at those fireworks."

"Oh, Sugar," she responded, "it *is* wonderful but not just because of that."

Then my mama, who struggled to make ends meet, declared with patriotic pride: "It's wonderful because my two dollars are in that statue."

We bring what we have to where we are. That's what life is all about. As we join together to do good, celebrations happen. We may not have a million dollars, but we may have two dollars to give to the life of a city and to the lives of others.

SHORT PAUSE *A Dilemma*

Does passing a person begging on the street spark an interior dialogue in us? Do we find ourselves in a dilemma between the "deserving poor" and our own personal financial security?

Taray, one of my sixth-grade students at the learning center, summed it up. "I get confused about sacrificing my money for the poor. Sometimes I have extra but keep it in case I need it later on. Other times I see a poor person who could use it, but she doesn't seem good enough to get it."

In Luke's Gospel, Jesus says it straight without dilemma or dialogue: "Give and gifts will be given to you. For the measure with which you measure will in return be measured out to you" (6:38 NAB). Jesus lets us know that the important thing is not *how much* we give or the debate in our heads about who deserves it or not, but *that* we give.

In Touch

*When I fall into the trap of making comparisons,
how might I use this occasion to understand different gifts
and abilities?*

Amidst the cornfields of Illinois, Doug struggled with his parents' divorce and his mother's second marriage.

To complicate the situation, his stepbrother was in my same sixth-grade class. Terrell was an outstanding student, accomplished athlete, and the apple of his father's eye. Doug found his studies a challenge, wasn't too keen on sports, and longed to play the flute and take art classes.

His family discouraged Doug's ambitions, deeming them unnecessary and counterproductive to an education. My parent-teacher conferences with them were dead-ends.

At the end of the school year, the family moved to Arkansas. With sadness I said good-bye. I had failed to convince Doug's parents of his talents and abilities. Even as adults, they had not learned one of life's important lessons: that each child has special gifts.

Two years passed. On a chilly March afternoon, I received a letter from Doug. Inside the envelope he had included a little plastic bag with small pieces of chalk. The letter began:

> *Dear Sister,*
>
> *Remember how you used to ask me to wash the chalkboard and ledges? Well, I saved some pieces of colored chalk and put them in a special box I decorated. They meant a lot to me because you had held them in your hands. Last month, I used some of them to create an art project. It won first prize. So now I am sending you some little pieces back, because I held these in my hands.*
>
> *This way we're in touch.*
>
> *Your student always,*
>
> *Doug*

As I closed the letter and resealed the plastic bag, I reflected on the hundreds of times I had written on the chalkboard. It took Doug to remind me that a teacher must write first on flesh, not slate—words that remain indelible and summon the power to shape a future.

MINING OUR FAITH, ENRICHING OUR LIFE

What personal differences have made me feel misunderstood and yet deepened my trust in God? In what specific ways might I reach out to those who suffer physical and mental diminishment?

SHORT PAUSE *Corner of the World*

The day after Hurricane Katrina hit, the old woman stood, destitute and hopeless, in front of the Superdome.

A newscaster asked her, "How are things?"

"I'll tell you how it is. A man over there's been callin' 'Jesus, Jesus.' I told him, 'Baby, Jesus don't live here no more.'" Then she sobbed.

I will never know what happened to this old woman. But I hope that when she saw volunteers clearing debris, neighbors sharing food and water, and strangers rebuilding homes, she found comfort because Jesus had returned to New Orleans.

SHORT PAUSE *Room for All*

One warm, spring day, some residents of The Boston Home, a long-term care facility for adults with multiple sclerosis, were gathering for a special religious program.

As residents began to arrive, we noticed that the room was filling up more than anticipated and that space was at a premium. In typical thoughtfulness, residents began shifting their wheelchairs to make more room available. It was a slow process and one in which every person had to be conscious of the other.

We were finally settled and just about ready to begin when a nurse asked if Jackie, very ill and confined to bed, would be able to attend. Her bed and IV fluid bag were rolled into the room and, once again, what seemed impossible, happened. With some pushing and squeezing and surprised relief, everyone fit.

As the room began to clear out after the service, one resident remained behind. Jane wheeled over and said, with that sense of satisfaction one has after solving a problem, "I think I know how life could work better. If everybody inched over and moved just a bit, like we did this afternoon, there would be room in the world for everyone."

Spicing her satisfied sigh with a smile, she mused, "Just imagine what would happen then!"

A Father's Son

ON ACCEPTING SHORTCOMINGS

How might the power of love soothe the pain we experience from others' shortcomings?

My third-grader Wynn, having an eight-year-old's belief in the magic growth of beanstalks and other living things, planted a sapling in his New York backyard that he hoped would yield a tree house. In the meantime, he spends his after-school hours in the cave he made. The cave is sheltered under a rock with side stacks of branches, twigs, and pieces of lumber. Wynn constructed this hideout for doing what he loves most: reading, sketching, and musing on dinosaurs.

After removing a book from his "bag of history," a name he has given his school bag, he studies one of these strange creatures with the eye of an artist and the precision of a scientist. His eyes hold all the details as he closes his book and begins to draw a stegosaurus.

This child's solitary life in his homemade cave is far more peaceful than life inside his house. His father is usually in an alcoholic stupor and his stepmother, ignoring Wynn, fusses over the year-old baby she considers her "real son."

Wynn has learned to fend for himself. He is usually a "ten-o'clock scholar," because he can't wake his dad for a ride to school; he skips breakfast, but knows he'll get a McDonald's hamburger for supper; he's unkempt because the washing machine is still broken.

Confused by his father's drinking and worried about his smoking, Wynn gave his dad a book from the school library about the dangers of cigarettes. He even posted a sign: "No drugs, cigarettes, or alcohol allowed in this house." He hasn't had any success but doesn't stop trying.

There had been a major fight between his dad and his stepmom, Wynn confessed through tears. He described the ugly details and then grew silent, exhausted by the painful memory. After a long while, he drew a deep breath, sighed, and began again.

"You know, even if my dad gets thrown out on the street and becomes homeless, even if he gets drunk and passes out on the sidewalk, I will still visit him every day and take him food. No matter what, I will always love my dad."

The dependent, frightened love of a son filled the silence.

Wynn reflected the immense conflict children often endure: the light and dark sides of parenting. Fathers and mothers long for the best in life for their children. Yet, their weaknesses can lead to their children's worst experiences of turmoil and struggle.

Because Wynn suffers from his parents' choices, he holds the love he has for his father as tightly as a teddy bear. This love rises above the domestic shouts, stupors, and neglect and becomes an amazing and saving grace.

———•◦•———

MINING OUR FAITH, ENRICHING OUR LIFE

What personal shortcomings have I acknowledged, asked forgiveness from God, and now trust to be dissolved into God's tender mercy? In what ways have I learned from my parents' shortcomings and allowed them to become grace and blessing for me?

———•◦•———

SHORT PAUSE *Under the Bed*

My neighbor Beatrice is terrified of storms. When the winds howl, the lightening flashes across the sky, and the thunder roars, she goes "into hiding." She never reveals her secret hiding place.

One summer afternoon, as we were chatting in the garden, I heard a distant peal of thunder. Forgetting her anxiety, I mentioned that a storm seemed to be brewing. She begged me to take back my words lest they become a reality.

Then she slowly began to share the source of her panic. When she was a child, her mother suffered from an extraordinary fear of storms. She thought that they signaled the world's end. Since her husband worked nights, it became her duty to protect their children from the inevitable. At the first sign of a storm's approach, she would awaken them, dress each one, and then, as a family, they would hide under the bed.

Beatrice smiled as she recalled that her husband wanted *their* children to enjoy storms. As they waited for them to appear on the horizon, Beatrice would head "backstage," but her husband and the children would huddle at the bay window. Counting down till "show-time," they would predict the number of sounds and fiery flashes. Their clapping and shouting continued until the last curtain call.

Life's full of storms that rumble along when we least expect them. In fear, we can hide under our bed, or, in faith, we can gather together at our bay window. Life has room for both.

SHORT PAUSE *Shooting Star*

With her head propped in her hands, third-grader Muriel was sitting quietly at her table in the classroom. Her friends were designing Mother's Day cards, complete with buttons and bows. I wasn't quite sure how Muriel would cope with this activity; her mother had died of breast cancer the previous September.

Distracted by questions of, "Sister, how do you spell . . . ?" and "What color goes with bright orange and light purple?" I had temporarily forgotten about Muriel.

When I glanced over, I saw that she was engrossed in her painting: a bold red and yellow streak arched over a star-studded black sky.

Muriel sashayed over and regally presented her masterpiece to me. Before I could say anything, she whispered, "Once my mommy and I saw a shooting star at the same time. The things you share with your mommy are the memories you keep."

Gazing upon the night sky this evening, I remember Muriel's generous wisdom and think of my own shared moments with *my* mother . . . memories that span across my life and light up the dark.

PART THREE
Experiencing God's Presence

As I am aware that all of life is saturated with God, this chapter explores a sense of the Divine in the persons and events of everyday life. Because we believe that "in God we live and move and have our being," as Paul speaks in the Acts of the Apostles, we accept life as gift, grace, and blessing. This openness to God's presence is the third practice of the abundant life.

In my own search for God's presence in everyday life, a childhood memory has become my mentor. Although some details have become fuzzy over the decades since, the message is still clear. This message continues to nudge me every now and then; providing me with a measuring stick for my life; challenging me to keep my eyes open; and urging me to dig my heels deeper into the holy piece of earth upon which I stand.

When I was about nine years old, my mother and I had "gone downtown," a common New Orleans expression that meant walking up and down Canal Street. This treat involved a trip on the St. Charles Avenue streetcar; a melted cheese sandwich at Woolworth's lunch counter; a chocolate soda from the fountain; and, best of all, the permission to select a small ten-cent bottle of "perfume" and pay for it myself with my allowance. I loved these special outings when I had Mama "just to myself."

As I chattered and Mama patiently listened, while enduring the smell of the overly sweet perfume, I noticed a double amputee on a large homemade skateboard. He lacked personal hygiene, from his greasy, matted hair and thick beard to his crumbled shirt and torn pants. His physical deformity coupled with his unwashed appearance became the object of my stare.

"Mama," I said too loudly, as I grabbed her sleeve for undivided attention, "look at that really dirty man over there. I bet he stinks."

Mama, whispering kindly, accepted my declaration without correcting me. "Sugar," she gently responded, "God is in that man."

"God?" I asked, totally mixed up. "Where? I don't see God."

Then Mama replied, "Just keep looking."

My quest began with those words. As a child, I would play a little game with myself, trying to find God in people and places. I would ask, "Where are you, God?" and would half-expect a hint, a whisper, a sighting. It was a sort of heaven and earth "hide and seek" that God always won. I never found God. I began to wonder if I ever would. My mother saw God everywhere, but she could not tell me how to do it and never even gave me hints. All she could counsel was "just keep looking."

Over the years, I have discovered useful attitudes in my own search to see God among us. Our success rate may not be high at first, but, over time and with resolute practice, these attitudes can lead us to experience the Holy.

One way to begin seeing God in others *is to avoid a preconceived notion of the "face" of God's coming in our everyday life.* We must forego expectations as to how God looks or acts and to accept that there are many divine disguises. If we look with the eyes of a critic at appearances as though life were a movie; if we give verdicts and sentences as though life were a courtroom drama; and if we give in to the temptation to judge why God is or is not present, we will run the risk of missing God. To encounter people as they are, without our personal evaluation and judgment, is to have a blessed inner vision. It is hardest of all to see the face of God radiating from our own mirror.

We will also overlook God's presence if we set the stage each day for the *form* in which God will come. It is not a question of what we have in mind for God. Rather, we open ourselves up to what God has in mind for us. So we live with expectation glowing in our hearts. This is a challenge, because we never really know God's plan until the day unfolds. When we surrender our predetermined idea of how God will come, we become sensitive to the new and unexpected ways God will break into our day.

We all know only too well those interruptions that disappoint and irritate us. When our plans are changed, we may even harbor little grudges and carry them with us throughout the day. If we are convinced that God is present in the change of plans, then something greater happens. We experience God's coming in the disappointment of a summer cold that keeps us in bed; in the extra mile of service that drives an elderly aunt to a hairdresser appointment; in the cancellation of a long-awaited job interview. How we thought the day would unfold and how it actually does are quite different. Despite our hesitations and disappointed feelings, we believe, with an unwavering inner conviction, that God came to us in a new way and in divine surprises.

We face another challenge for finding God everywhere: *we cannot depend on feelings to experience God's presence.* Although feelings can give us moments of profound spiritual insight, they are fleeting and are all-too-soon forgotten. How many of us have tried in vain to recapture a powerful experience of transcendence? True, feelings render us sensitive and grateful, but we know better than to place our whole experience of God on them. This is not to say that our feelings cannot lead us to God. It is, however, to say that our negative feelings say nothing about the absence of God, even though we might feel it as such.

Sometimes feelings make it easy to find God in the life around us. There are "Aha" moments when a sense of the Divine overpowers us. We remember times when we plucked peaches from trees bursting with fragrant fruit or watched crimson maple leaves twirling in the streets. We know the awe of parenthood that sweeps over us when we hear our child call "da da" over and over. We felt like we could reach out and touch, even taste, the Divine. Wonder and awe overwhelmed us as we realized that we experienced a tangible inkling of the Divine.

Then there are times when the sign of the Holy is subtle, as when we, with an eye on the sky, watch the sun playing peek-a-boo with rain clouds. Or when we see our breath on a cold winter's morning and marvel that God is as real as the air we breathe. At quiet times such as these, we brush against a hint of the Holy. These experiences bless us with an assurance that God indeed is with us.

But we must also be aware that feelings can seem to hide God's presence. We all experience those negative feelings that crop up in moments when God does not seem obviously present: the cranky neighbor who daily complains about the rabbits munching his garden vegetables; the airport delays that shorten the vacation we have been planning for a whole year; the anticipated bonus that was our due but didn't come. It is hard to realize that God is alive and well in the people, nature, and events of our less-than-perfect daily routine.

Even more, we may become cynical when we see the injustice and violence in our world: The number of homeless and unemployed persons increases; global warming causes glaciers to melt; hungry children die in natural disasters. Since God does not seem to be front and center, we wonder if God is anywhere at all. Or, even more sadly, we think that God is indifferent to the suffering and pain that is devastating our global community.

When our negative feelings surface, we can accept them as valid, but we should not let them take hold of us. We must move beyond the doubt, and even beyond a feeling of God's absence, and grasp onto faith. In times such as these, we know for sure that feelings are not the gauges of our belief in God's presence in the people and through the events of our daily life.

Unwavering faith is another spiritual stretch in our search to find God everywhere. This faith does not come naturally or overnight. It requires an expectant, disciplined attitude of mind that believes God is ever-present. It is a conscious decision to "keep looking" as we open ourselves up to God dwelling in each person and event of daily life. We are challenged to keep believing, especially when the search is devoid of blissful feelings and comforting assurances.

This faith plants our feet firmly on the holy ground of life in every situation. Faith sensitizes us to the hidden treasures under our feet: the very footsteps of God. Faith assures us that our good and gracious God walks the earth and spurs us on to accept that each engagement with our world can be an experience of God's presence. Faith convinces us to make nine-year-old Yuri's vision our own: "When I go outside and look around, God is always right in front of me."

Whether we feel God or not, faith intuits God smiling as we water our rose bushes; beaming through dawn's first light; sighing contentedly as we tuck our children in bed; and, hardest of all, looking at us in the mirror. Faith enjoins us to believe that God is right here, right now, present in this person, event, nature, and in my very self.

It is not always easy to find God in the people around us, in our daily routine, or within our very being. But, in spite of this challenge, it is our claim that "we walk by faith, not by sight," as Paul says in Second Corinthians (5:7 NRSV). This faith, sometimes joined to feelings, assures us that God's presence *this* day is as certain as the dawn. That is enough to keep us looking.

All the Same

*When have my personal sacrifices to alleviate the hardship
of others witnessed to God's care and presence?*

In the cool of the desert dawn, I would make my way down
to the dry river near our relief workers' compound. It was a
quiet spot where I could renew my inner energy and gather my
thoughts before facing the demands of the day. There, standing
before the expanse of sand, I would try to pray but would often
become quite restless. My thoughts would turn to water. Dreams
of turning on a faucet and putting my mouth underneath it would
captivate me. I would imagine tall glasses of ice water with a slice
of lemon. Then, the taste of a sand-filled, harsh, early morning
wind would break into my thoughts and bring me back to the
reality of drought.

On a morning such as this, I first noticed the Muslim woman.
She was further down the bank, standing with a regal bearing and
in rapt attention. I watched her as she stood immobile for long
stretches of time. I tried to imagine her musings and wondered
how long she had been in the refugee camp.

One day, she brought three children and an earthen jug with her. I watched her let go of the grasp of her two children's hands, take the jug from her head, and put it on the ground. Then, she removed the infant from her back. With grace and dignity, she lifted the child to the heavens. Then I knew. She was, indeed, asking for water, not for herself but for her children.

She returned the infant to her back and knelt down. Slowly, she began digging little holes in the sand. This went on for some time and, much to my surprise, she vigorously began scooping with a small, metal, spoon-shaped instrument. I realized she had found a water hole. Reverently, carefully, she was placing water in her jug. Little by little, she continued, bent low, as though in adoration.

Once in a while, she would dab a little water on the lips of her children and once, only once, did she dab her own. The right to water had become sheer gift.

I thought of my long showers, of running water while brushing my teeth, of washing less than full loads of laundry. How much water had I wasted over the years?

I left her there with her children and Allah, but I carried her in my heart for several weeks.

Then, one day, we met. I was canvassing the camp, going tent-to-tent, checking for children who were malnourished. Parents, giving up hope for a starving child, would hide their little one under a pile of rags in a corner of their tent in a gesture of waiting for death. Some mothers thought that only the stronger children had the right to eat. These parents needed our encouragement to bring even the sickest child to the feeding center.

Unknowingly, I passed Aisha's tent. She looked at me, and I recognized the woman at the river bed. We exchanged polite Arabic greetings, and then she spoke one word: "Aisha."

"Bridget," I replied.

Our smiles conveyed that now we each knew the other's name and because of that, we were bonded in relationship.

Our friendship did, indeed, grow. Each day we would meet when Aisha brought her children to the feeding center for hot milk and high-energy biscuits. We would smile at each other and gesture profusely in our attempts to converse. Little by little, she taught me a few simple Arabic words and learned a few English ones.

The months passed. Before long, my yearlong service in the refugee camp was coming to an end. I had mixed emotions. I knew I was going home to food, medicine, and water. I also realized that the children and families I had grown to love would continue to weaken under the desert sun, would walk miles to find water holes, would be hungry every day, and would die of malnourishment and disease.

On the day of my departure, I returned to the feeding center for the last time. One-by-one, I said good-bye through tears of frustration, guilt, and love. A sense of powerlessness gripped me as I surrendered the lives of these children to God.

With a heavy heart, I realized that I had not seen Aisha. Lost in this sad thought, I began my trek across the desert to gather my belongings for the trip to Khartoum. Suddenly, the sound of my name, heavily accented, reached my ears.

"Bridge, Bridge," a woman was calling.

I turned and saw Aisha, the regal woman at the riverbed, now racing barefoot across the hot sand. She had two children in tow and her baby, now strong and nourished, on her back. She threw out her arms in the nurturing embrace of friendship.

Then she took my hand, pressing a Sudanese pound into it.

Immediately, I recalled trying to change British pounds to Sudanese in London. The bank teller merely smirked and said, "Sorry. We don't deal in play money."

That Sudanese pound was Aisha's payment for a twelve-hour-day's work in the desert sun. Worth about fifteen cents in exchange, it was priceless to Aisha. It was all she had.

In Arabic, I told her no, and returned the pound.

She resisted. Although I could not understand her Arabic, her facial expressions and gestures toward the heavens conveyed her insistence and determination.

"Yes, Bridge. You take it. Whether I give it to you or give it to Allah, it is all the same. All the same, Bridge."

At that moment, I realized that Aisha had discovered wisdom in her life, so well lived. She saw no distinction between what we do for God and what we do to and for others. It is all the same.

I opened my hand to receive both the pound and Aisha's selfless and generous gift of love and farewell. Into this outstretched hand she gently and reverently placed the Sudanese money.

As I took it, I realized that as my call to Sudan began, so my stay there ended—with outstretched hands.

————

MINING OUR FAITH, ENRICHING OUR LIFE

What might change in my life if I truly believed that there is no difference between what I do for God and what I do for others? How could this lead to generous faith?

<hr />

SHORT PAUSE *Unwrapped Peppermint*

It was a sticky summer day. Life felt like the weather as I boarded the bus to the retreat center. As I slumped in my seat, I noticed a street person staring at me.

The stranger jiggled over, extending his unwashed hand. "Want a peppermint?" he kindly asked.

"Thanks, sir. But I've given up sugar for the year. You enjoy it."

When the bus approached my stop, a voice called out. "Miss, you're lookin' REEAALL good."

Life changed in a flash. I got off the bus with a dance in my step and a song in my heart. I don't know what made the difference: the offer of an unwrapped peppermint or the sweetness of being noticed. But one thing I do know: God always offers us a gift and a gaze.

———

SHORT PAUSE *Hurt Pieces*

Mr. Fulton, the first grade math teacher, was bellowing across the hall. I knew who was causing his frustration—Joey.

Something in Mr. Fulton's voice made me cringe. For a split second, I felt I was in Joey's place.

Later, in language arts during our story about crows, Joey suddenly began to caw. I hugged him and said, "Thanks, Joey. That's exactly how they sound." He hugged me back and smiled wide enough to cover a cornfield.

Cassie, an observant first-grader, whispered, "We got to make love out of people's hurt pieces."

Her words reminded me how healing happens—in love and in hugs.

A Church Lady's Holiday

*How do I feel when those in need want to ease
my life's burdens?*

It was a Thanksgiving etched in memory.

For several months, I had been living in Sandy Lick Hollow
in the hills of West Virginia, sharing life and lessons of the heart
with my mountain-folk neighbors.

Delena and Elam lived two miles deep in a hollow. The dirt
road, muddy, rugged, and often strewn with fallen branches,
made my trip there both a challenge and a risk. I often wondered
how they were ever able to get out, never mind how often.

"Home" was a ramshackle dwelling, hardly worthy to be called
a "house." It was there that Delena and Elam raised their five
children and a host of stray animals in need of shelter.

Their destitution was accentuated by cruel judgments and
a mountain prejudice. They were shunned by neighbors who
deemed them unfit and callously referred to them as "poor
white trash."

Early one evening in late October, Delena and Elam came to
visit for the first time. They had chugged their hour trip in a

borrowed truck, long overdue for a safety check. They climbed the stairs to the porch, one hesitant step at a time. I sensed their concern. I was certain that they had come for material assistance, and I began to mentally calculate how many potatoes, cans of beans, how much milk, wood, or coal I could reasonably spare.

Suddenly Elam's words broke my thoughts.

"We'd be rightly honored if you would join us for Thanksgiving dinner. You're a long way from home, and it's a family day. We're asking early 'cuz we'd like to plan."

Filled with uncertainty, doubt, and longing, Delena's eyes caught mine.

"I am delighted with your gracious invitation," I replied. "I'll be there."

"Bring nothing. Nothing at all," called Elam as they got back into the truck.

Thanksgiving Day arrived. It was cold but snow-free as I began the trek to the hollow and to a holiday dinner with friends.

Pity for their situation overwhelmed me as I entered their home. There was no water, no electricity, no indoor plumbing. Flattened cardboard boxes taped together formed the walls that encircled the family and kept the winter cold at bay. The coal stove, intended to heat all the rooms, actually heated only one.

The children squealed with delight when I arrived. They ushered me in to "sit for a spell" to warm up and to catch up, so I took my place close to the coal stove. Delena said it was good to feel the warmth of life and blessings on such a day as this.

"Come to the table," Elam invited.

We all gathered around, held hands, and offered prayers of thanksgiving for all we had been given—our ongoing friendship, enough food, the children, the creek and abundant well water, summer pole beans and sun-ripened tomatoes, purple irises on the hills and blue chicory along the roadsides, the wood for the stove—and all that was yet to come. Then we took our places.

As I looked at my place, I could see that Delena had neatly arranged the best plate in the house, a Mason jar glass, a spoon, and a fork. She, Elam, and the children shared the remaining two plates, three forks, and two mason jars.

My eye caught the decorations for such a festive occasion. Some sprigs from a pine tree spruced up an old jar. The cardboard walls facing me were decorated with pinecones and fir branches and held a boldly written message: "A big welcome to the church lady."

As soon as Elam offered me a plate with some sort of meat covered in oil, I sensed a challenge.

"Good, strong, wild meat," he said. "Been savin' it for just such a time."

I helped myself to the unidentified dish, knowing it couldn't stay on the plate and hoping it would stay down. I thought it best not to ask what made the meat strong and wild.

Then Delena offered me "the last greens picked before the frost got 'em all, and the mushrooms are from the summer. They been stored real good and should be fine."

I am sure she did not say "should be fine" in the emphatic way it sounded.

The meal went on. Eating, laughing, singing together a spirit-filled rendition of "The Old Rugged Cross" made thoughts of turkey, cranberry, and pumpkin pie oozing with whipped cream disappear into the cold air, and the reality of mystery meat and stale mushrooms find a resting place.

Before long, darkness began to set in and with it the time to take leave. It was the good-bye that I will never forget. Extending her hands, Delena took my hands in hers. Elam and the children surrounded me.

Delena began.

"We have somethin' to say before you leave. Hain't never, I mean never, has anyone done come to our home to eat with us. Not that we hain't invited them. But you came. And you came on Thanksgiving."

Then she paused, her eyes glistening with gratitude and penetrating mine.

"No," she continued, "it wasn't you. Today Jesus himself done come to our home, and we give thanks for the blessing of his presence. We don't have to go anywhere else to look for him 'cuz he is right here, before our eyes, inside our home. We look upon him."

I could say nothing. Delena and Elam, the poorest of the poor, the outcasts, had welcomed me as Jesus, had seen Jesus at their table and in their home. They knew that they were not born two thousand years too late. They needed neither angel choirs nor a star in the East to proclaim his presence. Like an awkward drummer boy playing his instrument, they worshiped Jesus with the best they had, having found him in a church lady far from home on a holiday.

MINING OUR FAITH, ENRICHING OUR LIFE

When have I humbly realized that someone saw Christ in me? How did this open my eyes to the beauty of sharing and to the witness of love?

SHORT PAUSE *Songbirds*

There's a Chinese proverb, "Keep a green tree in your heart and tend it gently so that birds will come warble in its branches."

What are the songbirds that nestle in the tree of your life? Do they show you how to rest in the niches of ordinary life's branches? Do they sing to you: *Go out on a limb for peace?* Maybe they urge you to glide through each day, one wing beat at a time.

Waiting in line at the grocery store or stopping at a red light provide blessed moments to listen to God in the warbles of our songbirds. Do we hear their symphonies calling us to harmony with creation, their choruses of justice and compassion, their chants of wisdom and wonder?

———

SHORT PAUSE *When I Grow Up*

It was the annual "What do you want to be when you grow up?" segment of the first-grade curriculum.

The boys I taught veered toward police officers, firefighters, and one livery driver. My girls saw themselves as mothers, nuns, teachers, and even a dancing nurse.

Molly, a reflective and reticent child, was keeping a low profile. Toward the end of the week, she simply stated: "I know exactly what I want to do when I grow up. I want to help everybody who's anybody or nobody."

There is nothing nobler than turning an act of giving into the art of living.

Work of Art

*What do life's unfinished masterpieces tell me
about God's work on earth?*

I never knew her name. She was a young child in Rome,
standing forlorn and cold outside the train station. In her arms
she carried a toddler, naked, dirty, and hungry. From time to
time this ten-year-old would glance lovingly at the toddler and
stroke her head.

Since I had spent a year in Rome, I knew the ways of the
street children. They would often distract unsuspecting tourists
in order to steal from them. From afar I studied this girl, as if she
were a great Italian work of art. Even in her unkemptness, she
radiated depth, dignity, and grace. I wondered if she was waiting
for a passerby or just waiting for time to pass.

I was not sure why I approached her, clutching my purse as
tightly as she grasped her sister. Our eyes met and I, surprising
both her and myself, offered my lunch bag. She put her sister
down, gently and gingerly took the sack, and began to unpack its
contents: bread, cheese, an apple, and a piece of chocolate. Her
eyes brightened, and I was pleased with my courage and charity.

The girl took a bite out of the apple and, much to my chagrin, began to repack the lunch. Feeling disheartened and wrestling with resentment I thought, *Why did I bother? The poor can be so choosy.* Putting the lunch on the ground, she picked up her sister. I knew she was leaving both it and me.

Then she looked at me with a smile as wide as the Coliseum. With tenderness, she held out her sister. Her eyes and her nod bade me take her. Reaching for her, I held her close.

In charity, a first-world adult had shared bread to feed a poor street child, and in return she shared life to nourish and nurture. The famous paintings and ornate monuments, the magnificence of Rome's churches, and the power of its history paled before this graced encounter. This child was life's masterpiece. Without a word spoken, she invited me to contemplate the canvas of a work in progress. Before God's work of art called a human life, the only response is reverence, silence, and love.

MINING OUR FAITH, ENRICHING OUR LIFE

When have I contemplated the face of God in a child? In what ways can I put aside my brush and allow God to complete my canvas?

SHORT PAUSE *Heaven vs. Earth*

"Let's change the subject to heaven," Robin blurted. For poets, preachers, and second-graders, heaven is such a fascination.

Samson, another second-grader, eagerly shared that, when his grandma died, her soul went to heaven and her body went in a treasure chest. Curtis said that heaven is the best place to go, so he didn't care when he died. Then he cautiously clarified, "Except not before Christmas."

Brendan remained silent. Concerned about his reticence, I asked him to share. "Heaven's a super place, but it's not like earth. Do you think I'll hurt God's feelings if I get just a little homesick?"

Enjoying heaven and missing earth—it's a tension that God can handle.

SHORT PAUSE *Watching and Waiting*

As I was sitting on a bench in the entrance of a crowded restaurant, I noticed how many people kept glancing at the clock, trying to estimate their party's arrival time or calculating how late their friends were.

What was even more noticeable was the bobbing of heads. Each time the entrance door opened, heads jerked up from menu reading, and eyes would rivet on the front door.

I wonder what would happen if we waited on God with such intensity. What if we studied the menu of our lives, quietly and intently? What if each time opportunity came knocking, we glanced up to look for God?

What if, once seated, we offered thanks and raised our glasses to welcome the God who, much to our relief, always shows up just in time?

Shell Seekers

ON AN ATTITUDE OF DYING

In what ways do I avoid thinking about death?

Crystal, who is eight, lives in rural Maine, under the spell of the ocean. Sitting on the rugged rocks, she smells the ocean in the air, feeling its breeze cool her face and mess her hair. Just she and Grampy.

She adores Grampy. He would meet her after school and together they would begin their explorations. Some days they were shell seekers; other days they were "snake-eyes," as he would say.

Grampy seemed to know everything about seashells: their names, shapes, and even their origins. But the way he held each one taught Crystal more. He would hold a shell reverently, marvel at its beauty, share his knowledge, then put it back in the sand. "It's home here," he would say.

It was the same way with snakes. In the late spring and summer, Crystal and Grampy would find little fields and begin their search to discover a new species, size, or color of snake. He taught her how to let them glide smoothly in her hands, like fish in the ocean. She laughed when her best friends said they were too busy to go snake hunting. She knew they were afraid.

One hot summer morning, Crystal discovered a new rock haven along the shore. "Just big enough for the two of us," she excitedly told Grampy.

"And the perfect place for sharing our secrets," he whispered with a touch of sadness in his voice.

They climbed together, safely nestling in the water-worn shelter. As the rocky fastness protected his heart, Grampy knew that he had to tell her. He was sick, he said. He had cancer.

Then he pointed out the horizon and said that beyond it were big ships. He knew that, even though he could not see them. Grampy asked Crystal to believe it, too. He reassured her that heaven's like that, real but unseen. He told her he would have a long time to glide peacefully in God's sea of love, just like fish and snakes. They held hands and sat a long time, the sound of the waves adorning the silence between them.

Three months later, Crystal came, downcast, into my classroom. "He's gone," she said quietly. Then she continued, "I think Grampy knew when God was coming, because he was real relaxed. Like when we were together at the ocean. I don't know when God got there to take Grampy to heaven, but Mommy knew. I'm sure he will always keep the present I gave him. I gave him all my tears to take with him."

I opened my arms and embraced Crystal, like the ocean around a jutting rock.

How often have I repressed, choked on, excused, fought, and hidden my tears? Somehow I would feel less adult, too emotional, and very unheroic if they would fall. Crystal reminded me that tears are a gift, given and received.

Like the tide, thoughts of Crystal roll in when I gaze at the ocean's horizon with the shells of loved ones' memories at my feet.

———•••———

MINING OUR FAITH, ENRICHING OUR LIFE

In times of loss and pain, how might I experience God's gentle nearness in my tears? How do I hear God's loving whisper in the seashells of memories?

————

SHORT PAUSE *Knock at the Door*

"Mr. Senabou will come soon for three loaves of bread," Sister Laurita told me. "Be sure to give him the freshest ones. He's walked a distance."

As I opened the door of our convent mission, I was completely caught off guard. When Mr. Senabou extended his hand, I saw tiny, ulcerated stubs instead of fingers. Mr. Senabou, severely disfigured and crippled, suffered from Hansen's disease. He was a leper, but none of the sisters had thought to tell me.

That day, admiration for my sisters in Senegal was carved in my heart. They saw people, not diseases; friends, not lepers. At the Last Judgment, these sisters will never have to ask, "Lord, when did we see you hungry?" My sisters saw Jesus every time they opened the door for Mr. Senabou.

SHORT PAUSE *Want a Drink?*

"Can I be first today to get a drink—pleeeease?" begged kindergartener Cian. "You always make me be last."

"When you learn to stay in your seat, Cian. And that's that." His daily nagging wore me out.

One day, he slid over. "I *am* staying in my seat. Why do I have to wait and wait for just a cup of water?"

At this, I was ashamed. In Sudan, I'd seen children digging in the sand for water. And here I was using water as a tool for classroom discipline.

"Cian, today you can go first and have *two* cups."

A few minutes later, rushing back and smacking his lips, he handed me his crumpled cup with a little bit of water and apple backwash. "Water is God's good stuff. You want some?"

I suddenly realized that I was thirsty, too.

Stuck in My Head

In what practical ways might I honor another's individuality?

Sasha was headed for a troubled adolescence of emotional outbursts and defiant behavior. She responded neither to my disciplinary action nor to positive reinforcement.

Repeated parental conferences were of little help. Her mother wondered how a child who had everything could lack anything. When I asked about boundaries at home, Sasha's father vaguely responded that he disciplined her appropriately.

Sasha wandered lost and alone in an impenetrable world where adults were not welcomed.

Over the months, my frustration with her steadily increased. My patience, as well as all the behavioral modifications objectively constructed by our counseling team, were exhausted.

In late March, Sasha again incurred a penalty for a rule infraction. Called to my office, she sauntered in, silently challenging me as she looked me squarely in the eye and asked me what I wanted. In a flash, I raised my voice and exclaimed,

"Nothing. I simply do not understand you. Nor do I want to. Now or ever."

Sasha winced. For the first time, a tear glistened that I noticed and she ignored. In a choking voice she responded, "Just because your eyes and ears are stuck in your head, doesn't mean you can't see and listen from deep in your heart."

Then she began to cry.

That moment, I understood. Sasha was a mystery. Deep, incomprehensible, unfolding, struggling—yearning to be accepted. I had made her into a problem to be measured, dealt with, solved, and controlled. Stuck in my head, I had failed to feel her heart from the listening place within my own.

MINING OUR FAITH, ENRICHING OUR LIFE

When have I gotten stuck in my head and failed to feel another's heart?
How might I balance a sense of mystery and the need for boundaries in my own life and in the lives of others?

———•◦•———

SHORT PAUSE *As Good as It Gets*

When children talk about God, they create a colorful mosaic.

Contemplative ten-year-old Jean Eva is grateful: "When I sit by the ocean, I always tell God he really does give us the best he's got."

Five-year-old Gia has a more practical view: "God and the Easter Bunny work together. Only God knows if you're really sleeping or just faking. Then he tells the bunny."

Benny, an eight-year-old, hints at God's mysterious side: "God uses us in all ways. It's called his plan. The problem is when he keeps it all a secret."

It's nine-year-old Curt, though, who holds the crystal piece: "God is as good as it gets."

Who is God for you?

———•◦•———

SHORT PAUSE *Daffodils and Stars*

On the first day of their spring semester class, most of Professor Ferdinand's theology students felt intimidated. They soon realized that their professor was also the author of their text. Realizing his students' apprehension, Professor Ferdinand began his lecture with a brief meditation to calm their anxiety.

Telling all one hundred students to close their eyes, he encouraged them to stroll the campus. "Feel the grass," he invited them, "now relieved of the burden of heavy snow, under your feet. Look around. Do you see a tiny tulip shoot inching its way through the ground in flowery expectation? Do you see a small daffodil, bobbing its head in springtime joy? Can you feel the rays of the sun zapping your winter spiritual bleakness? Does exhilaration bubble within you? If it does, then you have felt God."

Then he would quietly add, "Only if you can *feel* the God of the daffodils, will you be able to *discover* the God of the stars."

Shuffling Barefoot

Where is God in the darkness of tragedy?

There was one thing we could always count on. He was always home by 6:00 PM. After answering the usual, "Honey, how was your day?" he'd flop in his reserved La-Z-Boy chair. Worn out from his day's work, he would kick off his shoes and rub his bare feet, babying the calluses and fallen arches. Then he would stretch out his legs and lean back, relaxed and comfortable. This is what I loved to see the most. It meant that my daddy, Buster Haase of Haase's Shoe Store, could rest after a day kneeling at other people's feet.

For Daddy, feet were meant for shoes. He believed that the right shoes for the right occasion was one of those details that many people tended to neglect. He would shake his head when teenagers would spend their allowance on penny loafers for the next party, only to kick them off as soon as they arrived at the Sock Hop. He knew that the expensive high heels some women bought would have their special place under the office desk as soon as work began. More important, he could never quite understand why God, from the burning bush, told Moses to take off his shoes. Daddy would simply sigh and, I think, wonder what God must have been thinking.

Daddy was a master craftsman of his trade. He was convinced that health and happiness depended on a good pair of shoes. Patiently and gently, he would tie and untie laces, fitting as many pairs of shoes as were necessary to please a customer. Fiercely guarding the reputation of Haase's Shoe Store, he would rather discourage a purchase than profit from a sale with an improper fit.

Being meticulous about children's feet, Daddy, disregarding maternal preferences, would encourage a mother to buy Buster Brown shoes. He would enumerate the benefits of this oxford, then to the delight of her child, he would begin the singsong rhythm of its jingle: "I'm Buster Brown. I live in a shoe. That's my dog, Tige. He lives there too!" I loved to hear him render it and often marveled, with a young child's admiration, that a shoe had been named after my daddy.

As the years went on, I began to think that Daddy did live in a shoe, a tightly laced one with little wiggle room. Most of our conversations seemed unfinished, like hastily applied shoe polish that failed to cover scuffs. I could never understand the dynamic of our detached and distant relationship. Then, one evening, in one sentence, Daddy pieced it together for me.

Daddy came back from his World War II double tour of duty when I was two-and-a-half years old. During those years, he dreamed of the father-daughter bonding and counted the days until he would see me for the first time. But I, with toddler's glue, stuck to my grandfather with whom I had lived since birth. When Daddy returned, I would have nothing to do with this strange man. "Some scars of war can't be seen, only felt over and over," he dejectedly once said. I painfully sensed I was part of his wounds. Would we ever learn to walk in each other's shoes?

The night before I was to enter the convent, Daddy quietly told me that he thought being a nun would have lots of challenges. "No matter what, always remember two things: pick yourself up by your boot straps and keep a stiff upper lip." I saw his lip quiver as he handed me a buffalo nickel for good luck. He laughed and said, "No daughter of mine, nun or no nun, should ever be without money." Then he added, "I'll always watch out for you." With that teasing gesture and in those tender words, Daddy said good-bye to the daughter he had waited a war to embrace. In this farewell, a father-daughter conflict dissolved. But his personal battles were far from over.

On an October evening, the clock struck 6:00 PM, but Daddy didn't come home. The sound of the doorbell replaced the sound of his voice. Two police officers had come to say that Daddy was dead. In the locker room of the nearby golf course, he had put his socks and wallet neatly on a bench. Then he fired a single gunshot that ended his life.

Evening became night as a terrible darkness descended upon my mother, my four siblings, and me. It would be years before we could, each in turn, experience the dawn.

News of Daddy's death reached a local community of cloistered religious nuns, the Poor Clares. Going barefoot, except during the coldest days in winter or for errands outside the monastery, they would go to Haase's for footwear. Daddy would kneel at their feet, carefully fit their shoes and say he would send the bill later. He never did.

Unknown and unexpressed to each other, each sister of the community had decided, prompted by her heart, to wear to Buster's funeral the pair of shoes, no matter how old or worn, he had given her.

In a silent tribute to their friend who sold shoes for every occasion, barefoot sisters, each now shod in his legacy, would bid farewell. It broke their hearts to envision this man of golf shoes and wing tips shuffling alone and barefooted across heaven's threshold.

Gradually, I have come to realize that Daddy taught me more in his death than he ever could have taught me in life. His dying challenged me to look at life from the different perspectives of the triangular mirror used when trying on a new pair of shoes. Those angles revealed many reflections, many sides, and a gamut of choices.

Daddy's suicide taught me that one act does not determine the whole of one's life. Love shown, kindnesses rendered, sacrifices made, pain endured, worries borne—these constitute the essence of goodness and make a difference in the lives of others. A single act, in a moment of total despair, does not take this meaning or goodness away.

In my father's dying, I glimpsed the endless mercy of God. Our tender God is with us as a mother is with a sick and weak child. In the desperate experience of meaninglessness, God embraces and abundantly pours out both mercy and compassion. When God shares the pain of our intense personal suffering, our God weeps with us.

These sparks of love and compassion have transformed the tragedy of a suicide into a fire and passion to live well. Life has become a burning bush for me. In reverence and awe for the holy ground upon which I stand, I, like Moses, take off my shoes.

Daddy, the salesman of fine footwear and proper fit, with shoes for every occasion, slips his shoehorn into his pocket, winks knowingly, and approves.

MINING OUR FAITH, ENRICHING OUR LIFE

When I have a sense of hopelessness, what might help me believe that where I stand is holy ground? How might I handle a feeling of powerlessness when I see those I love suffer?

Gardens and Pine-Sol Floors

ON AN ATTITUDE OF BEAUTY

How might I see God's reflection under my feet?

For years I watched her clean house. With a bucket filled to the brim with a pungent Pine-Sol mixture and a soaked mop in hand, rags dangling from her apron, this woman would bend, kneel, stretch, and scrub, disinfecting corners, floors, and fixtures. After several hours of working with a boundless energy that others could only muster once a month, and with sweat pouring down her face, and calloused hands on her hips, she would survey her house-cleaning and sigh in satisfied pride. Her eyes would glisten and she would burst into a smile. As I observed her daily routine and knew that she gave every task her very best, I would wonder: *What is the driving force behind working so laboriously and yet so monotonously day after day?* It was a question I always wanted to ask my mother but never did.

Mama was a valiant woman, strong and independent. Yet she lived with both a profound and humble sense of her need for God and with a surrendered faith in divine providence. With her life shattered and her heart broken by my father's suicide, she courageously accepted all the effects of his death: the loss of their life savings and subsequent financial adjustments; the sale of her home; her search for employment; the struggles of tuition payments; the painful sorrow her five children endured. She was convinced that the measure of faith is how we handle things when it is tested, stretched, or seemingly absent. She would tell us that, as with the lilies of the field, God would tenderly care for us as we grieved and would give us the tenacity to rebuild our lives. The path ahead was unknown, but she trusted her God who seemed silenced by the gunshot. Mama never wavered in this conviction. Surprisingly, the years proved her right.

As time went on, I would envision my dream for Mama in her old age: financially comfortable, resting from her labors, enjoying life without worries, secure from sunrise to sunset. Life would return to her all that she had given and had accepted with fortitude and fidelity.

That dream, however, became a nightmare as, like the tide, Alzheimer's disease slowly flowed into Mama's life. I knew her agony of spirit as memory faded, confusion dominated, and all the household tasks, done so conscientiously over the years, became insurmountable. Her life was waning, and she, still cognizant enough to realize it, tried painfully and in vain to retrieve it.

Sadness would flood my heart as I would feel her anguish and dry her tears. After all her sacrifices and acceptance of tragedy, Mama sensed something was washing away the sand castle she had so meticulously built. She told me once that her life "was so far out there" and begged me to "help get it back." Her plea was a cry across the roaring of the waves, but I could only stand helplessly with her on the shore.

Over and over, I would ask myself: *What can I do for her?* Gradually, I began to realize that the greatest gift I could offer my beloved mother was to accept her as she was, not wishing her to be different or comparing her to the woman we once knew. "Rita T." (as I used to lovingly call her at times, referring to her maiden name—Rita Tangue) was my mother, and I believed that she would continue to both nurture and teach me even as the tide of Alzheimer's rolled in. And teach she did.

I watched her become a blessing for others. With the grace and charm of a fragrant and fragile gardenia blossom, which she loved so much, she was thankful for every act of kindness in the nursing home. Her smile, expressed through her blackened teeth, spoke the words she could no longer remember or express. Her life was a silent witness to a spirit of gratitude as refreshing as whiffs of Ajax Cleanser sprinkled in a kitchen sink.

Mama lived only in the present. Her past struggles were gone; her future worries, nonexistent. Perhaps, though, some questioning moments gently came back. I glimpsed that once when she told me she had "given all her life to God, both the good and the bad." Then, after labored thought, whispered, "Do you think it was worthy of him?" It wasn't the question that surprised me. It was that she asked it.

Toward the end of her life, she was hospitalized with a severe infection. It seemed like heaven's gate was slowly creaking open. Mama was silent and unresponsive as I sat by her bed. I held her hand, as white and frail as the gardenias she once tended, and the fragrant bouquet of her faith filled the room.

Suddenly and unexpectedly, she opened her eyes and seemed talkative. I, her daughter of sixty years, wasn't sure what to say or even how to converse. Then, remembering how she loved to garden, I softly said, "Mama, tell me about your yard."

Over a planting season's hour and in the halting bits and pieces of tiny seeds falling into the furrows of my heart, Mama shared her secret. "I never did my yard all at once," she began. "I did it piece-by-piece. I planted, weeded, watered. Finally, flowers would bloom. Then I would step back, look at it all, sigh in satisfied pride, and tell God that I had done what he wanted me to do on earth. I had created beauty."

Fixing her murky, watery eyes on me, she said, "Wherever you go, create beauty and then leave it behind." Then she fell silent and, as Alzheimer's tide rolled in again, she was awash in her own little world.

In that last conversation, I had the answer to my childhood's unasked question. That was the message of her life, the driving force of her house cleaning, the purpose of her yard: to create beauty wherever she went and in whatever she did.

In June 2005, in the month of lilies and gardenias, birdsong, lingering evenings, and summer sunsets, Mama lifted her tiny arm, now as thin as a blade of grass, in a last gesture of acceptance and surrender as God led this gardener into the Garden of Eden.

This valiant woman left behind a life of generous faith and love of the God who cared for the flowers of the field, her family, and for her. What Mama never realized was just how much, in all the seasons of her life, she mirrored her God of gardenias, gardens, and Pine-Sol cleaned floors.

MINING OUR FAITH, ENRICHING OUR LIFE

How might those with Alzheimer's disease and dementia teach us to live in the moment, trust in divine care, and bear witness to God's presence? In what ways can I create beauty and then leave it behind?

CONCLUSION

In these stories we have met men, women, and children living across cultural borders and close to home. We have sat at the ocean with a dying shell seeker, held a Gypsy child in our arms, and laughed over bus tickets and ladders. We have experienced the power of desert-baked tears of compassion and of a son's undying love for his father.

These people challenged us to cease searching "out there" for an elusive "more" in life. They reminded us that if we feel life has given us the short end of the stick, we measure incorrectly. They bade us to change our perspective by looking in the here and now for the abundant life. They are not people of theory but of practice: living their ordinary lives with attention to the present moment; accepting and trusting in divine care; and cultivating an expectant attitude of God's presence in their daily routine. Digging deeply, they have mined their faith and have responded with a witness that is open-handed, courageous, and lavishly reciprocal.

Remember Bird? Chewing tobacco under his favorite shade tree, he responds in disbelief, "Sissy, when a man knows that God is always on his side, how could he ever be lonely?" In the simple joy of blessed solitude, Bird assures us that all shall be well.

We catch ourselves off guard by our lack of attention to wonder when we hear Sister. Mary Xavier, at the age of ninety, quietly whispering, "I never tire of the vastness of the sky or the wonder of so many growing things." We ask ourselves how many times we even notice.

Buster, the salesman of fine footwear for any occasion, bids us heed God's counsel to Moses, "Take off your shoes. For where you stand is holy ground." We believe that, even through the tears and grief of untimely death.

In a rare moment of clarity that breaks through the thick clouds of Alzheimer's, Rita T. speaks her legacy. "Wherever you go, create beauty, and then leave it behind."

In her spirit, we tend our life's garden; spurred on by hope, we wait for our children to gather the blooms.

Sitting on life's porch together, these good neighbors remind us of the one conversation needed before closing this book. It takes place when we look in our own backyard, dig our heels deeply into the ground under our feet, and, smiling contentedly, realize that this *is* all there is to life. Convinced that it is, quite simply, *more* than enough, we then pass on the one story left to tell.

ABOUT PARACLETE PRESS

WHO WE ARE

Paraclete Press is a publisher of books, recordings, and DVDs on Christian spirituality. Our publishing represents a full expression of Christian belief and practice—from Catholic to Evangelical, from Protestant to Orthodox.

We are the publishing arm of the Community of Jesus, an ecumenical monastic community in the Benedictine tradition. As such, we are uniquely positioned in the marketplace without connection to a large corporation and with informal relationships to many branches and denominations of faith.

WHAT WE ARE DOING

Books • Paraclete publishes books that show the richness and depth of what it means to be Christian. Although Benedictine spirituality is at the heart of all that we do, we publish books that reflect the Christian experience across many cultures, time periods, and houses of worship. We publish books that nourish the vibrant life of the church and its people—books about spiritual practice, formation, history, ideas, and customs.

We have several different series, including the best-selling Paraclete Essentials and Paraclete Giants series of classic texts in contemporary English; A Voice from the Monastery—men and women monastics writing about living a spiritual life today; award-winning poetry; best-selling gift books for children on the occasions of baptism and first communion; and the Active Prayer Series that brings creativity and liveliness to any life of prayer.

Recordings • From Gregorian chant to contemporary American choral works, our music recordings celebrate sacred choral music through the centuries. Paraclete distributes the recordings of the internationally acclaimed choir Gloriæ Dei Cantores, praised for their "rapt and fathomless spiritual intensity" by *American Record Guide*, and the Gloriæ Dei Cantores Schola, which specializes in the study and performance of Gregorian chant. Paraclete is also the exclusive North American distributor of the recordings of the Monastic Choir of St. Peter's Abbey in Solesmes, France, long considered to be a leading authority on Gregorian chant.

Videos • Our videos offer spiritual help, healing, and biblical guidance for life issues: grief and loss, marriage, forgiveness, anger management, facing death, and spiritual formation.

LEARN MORE ABOUT US AT OUR WEB SITE:
www.paracletepress.com, or call us toll-free at 1-800-451-5006.

SCAN TO READ MORE

You might also enjoy...

Radical Hospitality
Fr. Daniel Homan and Lonni Collins Pratt
ISBN: 978-1-55725-891-5 | $9.95, Paperback

Deep within the heart of Benedictine spirituality is a remedy to hatred, fear, and suspicion: hospitality. True Benedictine hospitality requires that we welcome the stranger—not only into our homes, but also into our hearts. With warmth and humor, drawing from the monastic tradition and sharing personal stories, Pratt and Homan encourage us to embrace not only the literal stranger, but also the stranger within and the stranger in those we love.

AVAILABLE FROM MOST BOOKSELLERS OR THROUGH PARACLETE PRESS

www.paracletepress.com • 1-800-451-5006
Try your local bookstore first.

Use *Generous Faith* in your small group!

Generous Faith Participant's Guide
Sister Bridget Haase, OSU
ISBN: 978-1-55725-672-0 | $6.99

This Participant's Guide is like the headlight on a miner's hardhat. It illuminates your path as you travel to the cave of your heart to affirm the abundant life within you. Featuring reflection questions, thoughts for discussion, and suggested prayers, this guide is a handy tool for use in a friends' circle, in discussion and study groups, or alone during a time of prayer or spiritual retreat.